THE
TRAUMA
MYTH

ALSO BY
SUSAN A. CLANCY

Abducted

THE TRAUMA MYTH

THE TRUTH ABOUT THE
SEXUAL ABUSE OF CHILDREN—
AND ITS AFTERMATH

Susan A. Clancy, Ph.D.

BASIC BOOKS

A Member of the Perseus Books Group
New York

Published by
Basic Books, A Member of the Perseus Books Group
387 Park Avenue South
New York, NY 10016

Books published by Basic Books are available at special discounts for bulk
purchases in the United States by corporations, institutions, and other
organizations. For more information, please contact the Special Markets
Department at the Perseus Books Group, 2300 Chestnut Street, Suite
200, Philadelphia, PA 19103, or call (800) 810-4145, ext. 5000, or e-mail
special.markets@perseusbooks.com.

Designed by Pauline Brown

Library of Congress Cataloging-in-Publication Data
Clancy, Susan A.
The trauma myth : the truth about the sexual abuse of children—and
its aftermath / Susan A. Clancy.
p. cm.
Includes bibliographical references and index.
ISBN 978-0-465-01688-4 (alk. paper)
1. Child sexual abuse. 2. Sexually abused children. I. Title.
HV6570.C66 2009
362.76—dc22
2009032435

10 9 8 7 6 5 4 3 2 1

CONTENTS

A NOTE TO
THE READER

THIS IS A BOOK ABOUT CHILD SEXUAL ABUSE. It is based on interviews with adults, all of whom were victims of sexual abuse as children, who participated in research studies at Harvard University between October 1996 and August 2005. During the process of writing, my first priority was to protect the confidentiality of the victims discussed in this book. For many it was the first time they had spoken out about the sexual crimes against them. It was also very important to me to portray the reality of sexual abuse, the personality of the people who were abused, the complex interpersonal dynamics they faced both at the time of the abuse and in the aftermath, and the multitude of ways these crimes affect them throughout the course of their lives. In my attempt to reconcile both goals, I have opted to change the names of all the victims featured in this book and to either omit or modify any clearly identifying characteristics (such as age, birth date, place of residence, and specific occupation). That being said, the quotes throughout this book are taken verbatim from the actual victims' transcribed interviews. In this way I hope to respect and protect subject confidentiality while still accurately characterizing the humanity of these victims and the heartbreaking complexity of the crimes they experienced.

PREFACE

FALL 1996

FRANK GIRARD IS FORTY-TWO YEARS OLD. He has a steady job as a tax advisor, a wife of twenty years (his high school sweetheart), and three kids whose photos dangle from his key chain. Once a week he coaches a junior high school basketball team and at least twice a month he brings his family to church. Every March they all go to Sarasota, Florida, where Frank's invested with his brother in a time-share near the beach. On the outside Frank has it all—family, financial security, and good health—but on the inside he feels differently.

When Frank Girard was nine years old, something bad happened to him, something that he believes fundamentally damaged him, that powerfully and permanently changed how he felt about himself, who he is, his abilities, and his rights to success and happiness. For over three decades he has kept what happened a secret; he has hidden it completely from his wife, his family, and his friends and, as much as possible, from himself.

At the root of Frank's silence is shame. He suspects that what happened was his fault, that he brought it on himself, and as a consequence there "must be something wrong" with him—that it happened because he was in some way "aberrant." Not surprisingly, he does not want anyone to know, least of all the people that he is close to and who love him.

Despite Frank's efforts not to talk about what happened to him as a child, recent circumstances have made keeping silent increasingly difficult. He's been experiencing significant problems both at work and in his marriage—problems that he believes link back to his childhood experiences—and he suspects that resolving these problems will require reaching out for some kind of professional help or support.

• • •

ON A COLD, RAINY EVENING in October, Frank took the subway home from work, and he saw a copy of the *Boston Globe* on the empty seat next to him. As he idly skimmed the pages, an ad jumped out at him. The ad read, "Were you sexually abused as a child? Please call Susan for more information regarding a research study on memory in the Department of Psychology at Harvard University." Frank read the ad twice. Although his final destination was supposed to be Alewife Station, when the train screeched to a halt at Harvard Square, he got off. Fifteen minutes later he was outside the door of my office, soaking wet. Could he be part of the research study? Could it be now?

After more than three decades of silence, Frank was ready to talk.

• • •

AT THE TIME I WAS A GRADUATE STUDENT at Harvard University, just beginning the research project on sexual abuse that Frank read about in the paper. What Frank had to say to me was shocking. Beginning when he was nine years old, over a six-month period, he had sexual experiences with a middle-aged man who was a friend of Frank's family.

This was not the shocking part. Researchers in the sexual abuse field know that sexual abuse is common—that adults all too frequently exploit children for sexual purposes. What shocked me was how Frank said he reacted to the sexual abuse when it was happening to him. What gradually emerged, accompanied by long pauses, frequent sighs, half-finished sentences, and eventually tears, was that when the abuse was happening, Frank did not mind it. As a child, he loved this man, and he liked the attention this man gave to him. And sometimes what they were doing felt good. Occasionally he gave Frank baseball cards after the touching, and Frank looked forward to receiving them. When the man moved out of town, Frank felt upset. He missed him, the time they had spent together, and the attention he had received.

While I listened to Frank describe his reactions to the abuse, I understood why he felt ashamed and guilty about what had happened—why he felt "aberrant." Considering what I was taught and believed about sexual abuse, he was.

For over three decades, first the experts and then our communities have understood sexual abuse as a terrible experience for the child when it happens—as something invariably done against the will of a frightened child. But for Frank, when the sexual abuse was happening, it felt different.

Before Frank walked out the door of my office, he asked me a question. Since I was a researcher at Harvard and "studied these kinds of things," maybe I could help.

I told him I'd be happy to try.

For the first time in two hours, he looked me directly in the eyes. "What I told you . . . how common is this?"

At first I was relieved. This was a question I thought I could easily answer. I began, "Frank, childhood sexual abuse is very common. Approximately one in five children—"

But Frank interrupted me.

"No, not the sexual abuse part, I know kids get abused—for Christ's sakes it's in the papers all the time. . . . What I am asking is if other kids react to it like I did . . . you know, do what I did?"

Frank was referring to the fact that the childhood sexual experiences he had were not forced—because he had loved the man and enjoyed the time they spent together, Frank did not in any way fight or resist the sex. I had no idea how to answer his question. At the time, based on everything I knew about sexual abuse, everything I studied and was taught by professionals, I was sure Frank was an unusual victim, but I did not want to have to say this to him. I strongly suspected it was something he did not want to know.

So I decided to equivocate.

I said, "Frank, the field of sexual abuse research is relatively new. Maybe what you did—how you reacted to it—is common; after all, you were a kid, you cared about him, and you couldn't fully understand what you were doing, what he was asking from you, or what the consequences might be. Only time and more research will tell if your experience was common or not."

He seemed satisfied with the answer. But I felt terrible for not being totally straightforward with him.

• • •

THAT WAS MORE THAN TEN YEARS AGO. Today, after countless hours studying sexual abuse, reading and rereading research from the fields of psychology, psychiatry, law, criminology, and sociology, meeting with representative experts, and speaking with victims of sexual abuse—male and female, young and old, rich and poor—I do not feel bad anymore. As it turns out, I was telling the truth.

Today, despite their best intentions, some professionals in the sexual abuse field have developed and fostered major misconceptions among the general public about this terrible crime—what it really is and how victims react to it. In their well-meaning efforts to raise awareness that sexual abuse is damaging and is never the child's fault, they have chosen to emphasize characteristics and dynamics of abuse (such as trauma, fear, violence, force, and threats) that do not characterize the experiences that most victims have. As a consequence of this misplaced emphasis, professionals ignore and the public misunderstands the concerns, worries, and fears of millions of victims—people like Frank. These are instead overlooked, minimized, and denied.

In the current cultural climate, telling the truth about sexual abuse—directly addressing what actually happens and how victims react to it—is difficult. Many professionals and victims' advocates in the sexual abuse field worry that doing so will result in society's blaming the victims or questioning the harm sexual abuse causes. But these worries are unfounded. Sexual abuse, as I will discuss at length in this book, is never the victims' fault, and it most certainly damages them, but not for the reasons many of us have been led to believe.

It is often said that advocacy is best aided by truth. In this case, not only will facing the truth about sexual abuse set victims free from the chains of guilt, shame, and secrecy that bind them, but it will help criminal and legal authorities better identify and punish the perpetrators, mental health professionals develop more effective treatments, and parents better protect their children from becoming future victims of these vile and, to date, outrageously common crimes.

Introduction

CHILD *SEXUAL ABUSE*—a term mental health, legal, and criminal professionals commonly use to describe sexual experiences between adults and children—is astonishingly common. According to epidemiological data, based on randomly sampled, representative populations from the United States, gathered and analyzed using advanced and sophisticated social science research methods (by researchers with no apparent political or financial agenda), about one in ten men and about one in five women in the United States today has had a sexual experience (ranging from genital touching to oral-genital contact to anal or vaginal intercourse) as a child with an adult (someone over eighteen).[1] This translates into about forty-five million Americans. (Because people interviewed by researchers might not admit they were abused, many agree that these numbers are likely conservative).[2]

We have many explanations for the frequency of this crime. Some sociologists talk about societal deficits in information about sexual behavior. Mental health professionals talk about the need for more research and funding for child maltreatment prevention. Many feminists highlight women's subjugation in a patriarchal society. Religious conservatives have argued that sexual abuse is an inevitable side effect of an increasingly sexually liberal society, while some religious liberals posit that it stems from the sexual repression of priests. More than a few people I have bumped into have seemed to believe it results from the world's becoming increasingly immoral, from the irretrievable break down of social norms. An older woman sitting next to me on the bus recently summed up this perspective: "This generation is going to hell in a handbasket."

Explicit or implicit in these explanations is the underlying assumption that there is something unique about the present, that something specific about today's time and culture allows so much abuse to occur. But this is not the case. According to the same body of solid data I mentioned earlier, analysis of abuse rates by generational cohorts indicate that high rates of sexual abuse have been fairly constant over the last century.[3] It was common when our great-grandparents were alive, and unless we do something drastically different, it will be common when our children's children are born.

Not only is sexual abuse common, but no one is safe. Prevalence rates do not vary much across socioeconomic strata: Rich kids get abused just as often as poor kids, black kids as often as white, college grads as often as high school dropouts.[4] To makes these findings less abstract, go to any playground in any city or town in America and pick out five kids. Odds are one of them has already had a sexual experience with an adult or will have one before he or she hits puberty.

This "equal-opportunity" nature of sexual abuse has a lot to do with the fact that the vast majority of abusers (about 90 percent of them) are men we know and trust—family members, friends, teachers, sports coaches, camp counselors, piano teachers, rabbis, and priests.[5] The notion that most sexual abusers are weird and sick strangers (the "bogey man theory") is plain wrong.[6] Your average abuser is not a stranger or some convicted criminal staking out your house: It is someone you know, someone you respect and trust, and someone you'll most likely be happy to let in.

Not only is sexual abuse common, but it is damaging to those who experience it. Adults who were sexually abused as children (compared to people who were not) report a startling range of problems, including, but not limited to, mood disorders (like depression), anxiety disorders (like posttraumatic stress disorder), personality disorders, relationship and sexual problems, eating disorders, self-mutilation, alcohol and drug abuse, and even psychosis.[7] Although no specific pattern of signs or symptoms exists—not every victim is affected in the same way to the same degree—analysis of data from both clinical and nonclinical samples reveals strong and consistent associations between the experience of early sexual contact with an adult and a host of adverse adult outcomes. The most conservative synopsis of the situation would be that sexual abuse is a significant risk factor for a wide range of adult psychological problems and disorders.[8]

Not surprisingly, health professionals in the fields of psychology and psychiatry have devoted an intense amount of time and effort to helping victims cope with, and recover from, the psychological problems they report in the aftermath of sexual abuse.

In the same way as physicians approach the treatment of medical problems, mental health professionals believe that the best way to help patients suffering from psychological problems is to establish the root cause—the precise mechanism behind the problems. By establishing the precise nature of the cause, they can better treat it. So what is the precise nature of the psychological pain and problems victims report in the aftermath of sexual abuse?

The answer might sound like a no-brainer: If you experience psychological distress after sexual abuse, then the sexual abuse must be the cause. But it is not actually that simple. What, specifically, about the abuse has triggered the distress? Does it have to do with objective characteristics of the abuse (for example, how many times it happened or whether penetration was involved)? Does it have to do with subjective characteristics about the abuse (how painful, frightening, or shocking it was)? Perhaps it has less to do with the actual abuse and more to do with, say, the particular child (how old he or she was and how genetically predisposed to long-term psychological problems) or the environment the abuse occurred in (one characterized by poverty, physical abuse, or neglect). Maybe it has to do with the cognitive or social consequences of the abuse (how the victim's family or health professionals handled it or how the victim understood or conceptualized it later on in life). There are numerous ways to understand how and why sexual abuse damages victims. For decades, however, the main focus has centered on one—the incident itself.

The theory developed in the late 1970s, which sexual abuse experts accepted widely in the 1980s and today remains almost uncontested in the fields of psychiatry and psychology, is referred to as the traumatic stress (or traumatogenic) perspective.[9] In a nutshell, the idea is that sexual abuse damages victims not due to the particular nature of the victim, the environment, or the consequences of abuse but to the abuse experience itself. Sexual abuse damages victims, the theory goes, because it is a traumatic experience for the child when it happens.

Now, the word "trauma" means different things to different people. My cousin returned from service in Iraq and reported that getting shot at in the desert was traumatic. A friend ran over a frog while she was mowing the lawn and told me that seeing the animal die in front of her was traumatic. My colleague tells people that quitting smoking has been traumatic. A student just walked into my office and told me that studying for his exam has been traumatic. However, the way professionals in psychology define a traumatic event is clear: It is either objectively life threatening when it occurs (like getting shot at) or subjectively results in the same kind of intense fear, horror, or helplessness that objectively life-threatening events arouse.[10] According to the dominant theoretical framework, sexual abuse, like other traumatic experiences, damages victims because it is a frightening, horrifying, overwhelming, or painful event when it happens.[11]

The exact manner in which professionals believe that trauma results in long-lasting harm is complicated. Basically, the experience of psychological trauma causes extreme, unnaturally high levels of neurobiological arousal in the victim, arousal so extreme that it becomes toxic: It destabilizes the victims' neurobiology, leading to long-term emotional, behavioral, and cognitive dysfunction and, in some cases, even to brain damage. In other words, trauma can set off a chain reaction in the nervous system that influences levels of hormones and neurotransmitters and can impact the brain. Traumatized brains may have dysregulated systems poorly equipped to handle subsequent psychosocial stressors. In short, traumatic events produce profound and lasting changes in physiological arousal, emotion, cognition, and memory.

The traumatogenic model encompasses three basic assumptions. First, as I have already discussed, trauma is the central concept used to explain the long-term effects of child sexual abuse.[12] Second, the pathway through which the trauma of sexual abuse affects well-being is direct; that is, the emotional disturbance induced by the trauma of sexual abuse persists across long stretches of time. Thus, although victims report different negative outcomes in adulthood as a result of sexual abuse, all are symptoms of a lingering psychological disorder, the etiology of which is traced directly to the original sexual experience. As Lenore Terr, one of the foremost experts on the harmful effects of childhood sexual abuse, explains,

> Like childhood rheumatic fever, which causes a number of conditions in adulthood ranging from mitral stenosis to subacute bacterial endocarditis to massive heart failure, childhood psychic trauma leads to a number of mental changes that eventually account for some adult

character problems, certain kinds of psychotic thinking, much dissociation, extremes of passivity, self-mutilative episodes and a variety of depressive and anxiety disturbances. Even though heart failure and subacute bacterial endocarditis in adulthood look very different from one another and demand specific treatment, their original cause—"the childhood rheumatic fever"—gives an organizational pattern to the physician's entire approach. Every good internist knows how to obtain and assess a history of rheumatic fever. Thus just as rheumatic fever causes lots of problems, childhood sexual abuse causes lots of problems.[13]

The third assumption embedded in the traumatogenic framework is that child sexual abuse experiences fall on a continuum of severity that describes the level of stress induced and predicts the extent to which the child will suffer long-term negative consequences.[14] (The more traumatic the abuse was when it happened, the more acute the long-term negative outcome.) Put another way, the degree of traumatic stress experienced during the sexual experience best accounts for variation in long-term adverse effects. As Judith Herman, a psychiatrist at Harvard Medical School, states in her influential book *Trauma and Recovery*, "There is a simple, direct relationship between the severity of the trauma and its psychological impact." Accordingly, if a victim today reports psychological problems in the aftermath (as they usually do), the assumption is that the sexual abuse, when it happened, was a horrific experience—it was frightening, shocking, and overwhelming.[15]

Although increasingly many professionals and researchers in the sexual abuse field acknowledge that other factors not specifically related to the abuse might have something to do with harmful consequences, the main emphasis of much of the research has been firmly on the abuse. For at least three decades, the notion that the effects of sexual abuse flow from their traumatic character remains largely unchallenged.[16] Any sexual contact between children and adults is understood to be invariably awful for the child—an experience characterized by force, oppression, fear, and helplessness.

Not surprisingly, the trauma theory of sexual abuse has had a profound effect on how professionals talk about and describe sexual abuse. By far the most popular conception of the effects of adult-child sexual contact envisions the experience as the presentation of a noxious stimulus to a child, one that immediately produces adverse emotional responses. If you Google "child sexual abuse," as hundreds of thousands of people do every year, the American Academy of Child and Adolescent Psychiatry website is among the first returned for public access. The main page concerning child sexual abuse clearly states, "No child is psychologically prepared to cope with repeated sexual stimulation. Even a two or three year old . . . will develop problems resulting from the inability to cope with the overstimulation."[17]

Today, sexual abuse is very rarely described without the word "trauma" or without the implication that the experience involved fear and violence. Treatment centers are referred to as trauma centers. Sexual acts against children are described as "sexual assaults" or "violent encounters." In the words of Lenore Terr, child sexual abuse is a "horrible external event in childhood . . . rendering the young person temporarily helpless and breaking past ordinary coping and defensive operations."[18] Another tremendously influential researcher, Denise Gelinas, states, "There is little doubt that abuse constitutes a major trauma for the child, one which confuses and profoundly threatens. . . . The most predominant reported affect is fear."[19] Judith Herman writes, "At the moment of trauma, the victim is rendered helpless by overwhelming force. . . . The common denominator of trauma is intense fear, helplessness, loss of control and threat of annihilation."[20]

Sexual abuse, according to the standard diagnostic system used by physicians and psychologists (the DSM IV), exists in the same category of traumatic events as combat, rape, and natural disasters. As a consequence, many researchers studying the psychological impact of sexual abuse do not even bother to ask victims detailed questions as to whether the experience was traumatic when it happened; they just assume it was. Like rape or combat, sexual abuse automatically "counts" as a traumatic experience. If a victim of sexual abuse reports psychological damage in the aftermath, it is automatically assumed that the damage is a function of the degree of trauma the victim experienced during the abuse. In fact, the assumption of trauma is so inculcated into most professionals that if a victim does not report the abuse as a horrific experience when it happened, they often assume that the wrong questions were asked or the victim is misremembering the actual events.[21]

Naturally, what professionals specializing in sexual abuse and trauma believe, research, and write about is communicated to the general public. The trauma conceptualization of sexual abuse has, in the words of the medical historian Ben Shepard, been "vectored into society" and impacted enormously how it is presented in the media and subsequently understood by all of us.[22] Books about sexual abuse targeting victims typically open with such passages as,

> It is about the silence of nights spent holding in screams, holding back tears, holding in one's very self.[23]

> If you are reading this book it is because you remember the terrible and frightening experience of being sexually abused.[24]

> Why don't victims share their secrets? Because of the cycle of rape, shame, and unshared, unshareable torment.[25]

The Courage to Heal, first published in 1988 with a twentieth anniversary edition still selling well, perfectly exemplifies this trauma positioning. It is, without a doubt, the book most widely read by victims and cited by professionals. Continual references to trauma occur throughout this five-hundred-page tome, with words such as "blood," "rape," "sodomy," "terror," and "pain" used to describe the sexual abuse. Victims who read it are continually told that even if they feel otherwise, what happened to them was done against their will. According to the authors, the abuse was forced upon them; they were "utterly helpless" and "raped against their will."[26]

For thirty years the topic of sexual abuse has resulted in a steady stream of activism, public concern, and media attention having to do with topics such as abuse in day care centers, recovered memories of sexual abuse, celebrity abuse experiences both as victims and as abusers, and most recently the sex scandal in the Roman Catholic Church. To highlight the influential place the trauma model has in our understanding of sexual abuse, virtually every commentator shares the view that the sexual abuse was horrific when it happened and, as a consequence, profoundly damaging to the victim. Not surprisingly, when we read about sexual abuse in the news, watch a feature about it on TV, or witness it in the movies, it is almost always in the context of lurid, sensational stories having to do with subjects like the rape of choir boys by pale, wet-eyed Catholic priests, Internet stalkers luring young children for sex through their e-mails, international sex trafficking of young Latinos and Brazilians, and the rape of infants in day care centers. In *Mystic River*, an Academy Award–winning movie based on a book of the same title, strangers kidnap a young boy and sexually abuse him in a basement (this is a movie often shown at "kickoff" events when communities raise awareness about sexual abuse). Indeed, available cultural scripts foster and support the notion in our culture that sexual abuse involves fear, force, and coercion.

• • •

AS A GRADUATE STUDENT AT HARVARD in the 1990s, I never thought to question the trauma conceptualization of sexual abuse. Why would I? First of all, it made sense. To me, as for most of us, sexual abuse is a painful topic to think about. The idea that adults use children for sexual purposes is, quite frankly, morally and physically revolting. I assumed child victims would feel the same way.

Second, experts in my field had taught me to think this way about trauma. The trauma theory anchored the vast majority of research on sexual abuse. Why would I question it? I was repeatedly assured that psychology was a science. And the cardinal rule of science is simple: Believe only what the facts justify.

Science concerns the pursuit of truth. The pursuit of truth requires clear thinking, solid reasoning, logic, honesty, rigorous argument, and especially evidence. After years of having the importance of establishing one's beliefs on objective evidence drilled into me by people in my field, I assumed that an endorsed theory would be just that. It never once occurred to me to think otherwise. I trusted my field and its adherence to the scientific process.

On top of it all, not only were experts in the field telling me that sexual abuse is traumatic for the victims and that this trauma relates directly to the long-term psychological damage so many report, but they were telling me it was so traumatic that some victims would repress memories of their experiences until later in life. The levels of stress the victims experienced while being abused were suspected to be so high that they severely compromised an area of the brain called the hippocampus, which is responsible for processing and storing memories. As a consequence, the victims would be unable to remember what had happened to them. According to this perspective, victims sometimes report forgetting what happened to them and then remembering years later because the abuse was extremely traumatic when it happened.[27]

Although Sigmund Freud and his close friend and collaborator Josef Breuer first developed this concept of repression over a hundred years ago,[28] it only exploded into our cultural awareness in the early 1990s. All over the country, people began to talk about sexual abuse and to "recover" memories of their own. Celebrities came out on national TV to share their stories; nursery schools were shut down due to reports of sexual abuse; the FBI had to start an investigation about alleged recovered memories involving not just ordinary sexual abuse but sexual abuse involving satanic cults.

Many professionals in the field of sexual abuse endorsed the concept of repression, but some, including members of my department, did not. Skeptics like Daniel Schacter, at the time the head of my department and one of the world's most influential memory researchers, and Richard McNally, my advisor and a renowned expert in posttraumatic stress disorder, noted that according to a large body of laboratory and real-world data, traumatic experiences are usually remembered all too well; that is, emotional arousal at the time of an event's occurrence actually fosters the consolidation and subsequent accessibility of one's memory of it.[29] So why, if sexual abuse was traumatic, would victims forget it? Further, why were only sexual abuse victims repressing and recovering their memories? Why did victims of other types of traumatic events (like combat or prison camp confinement) not do it as well? Experts in the trauma field, such as Judith Herman, Bessel van der Kolk, and Lenore Terr, explained that there was something unique about the trauma sexual abuse victims experienced.[30] However, what specifically that something might be was not particularly well specified.

• • •

WHEN A PROJECT EMERGED that would address this issue, that would allow me to interview sexual abuse victims and collect data on just how traumatic the sexual abuse was, I jumped at the chance. It seemed so simple. All I had to do was find sexual abuse victims, ask them questions about what the experience was like when it happened, and then test the hypothesis that the more traumatic the sexual abuse was when it happened, (1) the more psychological damage victims would report in the aftermath, and (2) the more likely they would be to repress their memories. Both hypotheses made sense: I just needed to collect the data. In fact, they were so straightforward I was surprised the research had not already been completed and reported.

Before the study began, other graduate students asked me if I was worried about engaging in this kind of research. Did I not think it would be painful to talk to victims, to listen to their stories? Did I not want to pick something less difficult to do with my time? But I was naïve. I did not think so. Everything I had already done as a graduate student was psychologically painful (interviewing schizophrenics, the suicidal, and alcoholics), so how could this be any worse? Comparatively, I felt optimistic. After all the years of research, it seemed like our field was never going to cure schizophrenia, depression treatments did not always work, and getting alcoholics with a genetic marker for alcoholism to stop drinking was proving extremely difficult. This project was different. Based on what I had read, I felt that over the previous twenty years, the field had made progress for victims of sexual abuse, that for the first time in history, social and professional attention had been seriously mobilized toward this important topic. So I was thrilled to be part of it. I was certain that research like this was really going to help us solve problems and answer questions for victims.

My biggest concern was finding sexual abuse victims who would agree to come in and talk with me. It

was not going to be pleasant for them—they were going to have to answer detailed and personal questions
about their experiences—and I certainly did not have
much to offer them in return for their time.

Many scholars in the sexual abuse field told me that
the best way to find subjects would be to look for them
in the offices of psychotherapists specializing in the
treatment of sexual abuse. It would be easy to locate
victims that way.

But here was the problem. According to data, most
people who are sexually abused do not go to therapy to
talk about what happened to them. By choosing to interview only victims in therapy, I would be using a biased sample.

I decided to cut down on the bias by running an ad
in a medium where as many people as possible from the
general population would see it. I decided to run ads in
the *Boston Globe* (and eventually other major newspapers in the greater Boston area).

My concerns about finding sexual abuse victims
willing to talk to me turned out to be unwarranted.
When I came into work the day I first ran the ad, I already had over fifty messages waiting for me. It turned
out I would have no trouble connecting with brave and
generous sexual abuse victims in the general popula-

tion who would participate in research studies about their experiences.

Over a ten-year period, more than two hundred men and women participated in this and similar research projects pertaining to sexual abuse with me and with my colleagues at Harvard University (my sample comprised approximately 65 percent women, 35 percent men). Every single one of them was sexually touched as a child by an adult. By legal, professional, societal, and Harvard standards, they clearly met the criteria for victims of sexual abuse. Among the sample was the CEO of an Internet start-up that had just gone public (he was worth $62 million), a minor-league baseball player, a parolee who had just been released from a five-year prison stint for drug trafficking, a heroin addict in withdrawal who shook throughout our discussions, a stunning runway model, two Ivy League computer geeks working on a NASA-funded research study, an artist working on her first gallery show opening in New York, a woman living with her dog out of her Dodge Bronco, a dowager from the Back Bay whose husband had just left her for a man after fifty years of marriage, a litigation attorney who brought his own consent form for me to sign, a teenager with a lip piercing and a large tattoo on the back of her neck who was contemplating emancipation from her foster family, and more. They were a diverse group, but they shared two very important characteristics.

The first I expected: Almost every victim I spoke with reported that their childhood sexual experiences had damaged them. As the sexual abuse research I was familiar with predicted, they commonly experienced symptoms of psychological disorders (for example, depression and posttraumatic stress disorder). Although not all met criteria for actual psychological disorders, most reported multiple adverse effects from the abuse. They believed that what happened to them had negatively affected their lives and their relationships with others. In addition, forgetting sexual abuse (alleged repression) was not uncommon: I had no trouble finding people in the general population who reported periods during which they did not remember their sexual abuse.

The second commonality between the victims I did not expect. In striking contrast to the assumptions of the traumatogenic model, whatever was causing the psychological and cognitive damage these victims reported had nothing to do with trauma; very few victims reported any fear, shock, force, or violence at the time the abuse occurred.

1

What Was It Like
When It Happened?

*"I wondered why would anyone
want to touch me there. . . . It didn't seem right,
but I wasn't sure why."*
—ALEXANDRA, THIRTY-EIGHT YEARS OLD,
NURSE PRACTITIONER, MOTHER OF THREE

ERIN TAYLOR WAS THE FIRST PERSON to call the day my initial advertisement ran in the paper. According to my voice mailbox, she called at 5:15 in the morning. When I connected with her, she said she was not sure she met the criteria for the study.

"Okay," I said. "Were you sexually abused as a child?"

"I'm not sure," she said.

Not sure? (How could you be not sure? I wondered.) I rephrased the question. "Did an adult, someone older than eighteen, have sexual contact with you before you reached puberty?" Without hesitation, she said yes. After we discussed the details of her abuse and the research study, she agreed to participate, and we scheduled a time for her to come to my office to be interviewed.

Erin showed up for her interview early, carrying a latte from Starbucks, looking like a movie star. She was tall and thin, with long, shiny, blond hair, wearing a beautiful, fitted, cream pantsuit, crocodile-skin three-inch heels, a Cartier watch, and diamond studs. She had perfectly sculpted eyebrows. I was acutely aware that I had just rolled out of bed and was wearing the exact same beige sweatshirt and Gap relaxed-fit jeans I had worn the day before.

Erin briskly shook my hand, sat down, crossed her long legs, took out a leather eyeglass case from her Coach satchel bag, carefully removed a tiny pair of gold-wire-rimmed spectacles, rested them elegantly at the end of her refined nose, and began to carefully read the consent form I handed to her. She appeared calm and totally composed.

Erin had a couple of questions regarding subject confidentiality; it was very important to her that no one ever know she had participated. I stressed how the information she gave me might be used in scientific papers or books, but that all identifying features, like her real name, age, and occupation, would be changed so that no one would be able to identify her. In addition, she was not thrilled about the tape recorder. Was it really necessary? I thought it was. I would be transcribing these interviews, and I wanted to make sure that what these victims said to me was thoroughly and accurately recorded.

After she signed the consent form with her own fountain pen, I offered her some Munchkins I had brought with me from Dunkin' Donuts. She declined politely and looked at her watch. "We have one hour and forty-nine minutes left. Shall we begin?"

I turned on the tape recorder.

I collected background data about Erin. She was single and twenty-eight years old. She grew up in a wealthy suburb of Boston. She had one younger sister, and her parents divorced when she was very young. She had attended an exclusive private school, gone to an Ivy League college where she majored in finance, worked on Wall Street as a financial analyst, and received her MBA from a top-ranked business school. For the past two years she had worked for a Boston consulting group and traveled on business three days a week. In her own words, "In essence, I live out of my suitcase." She had no children, was not religious, was physically healthy, and had never gone to see a psychologist.

It was time to begin talking about the actual abuse. I explained to her that as per the interview protocol, I would start by collecting information concerning the objective characteristics of the abuse: what kind of abuse had occurred, who the perpetrator was, how old she was at the time, and how many times it happened. She nodded but warned me that this might be difficult for her as she had never told anyone about the abuse before. This took me by surprise. I wondered why. I also wondered why she wanted to open up after so many years of silence. She seemed to sense my confusion because, without my having to ask, she told me that she thought "it might feel good to talk about it after all these years" and the fact that she "didn't know me" and "wouldn't have to ever see me again" made "participating in this research study appealing."

Considering she said she had never talked about the abuse before, the interview went smoothly. She understood all the questions and answered them succinctly and clearly with no hint of emotional distress. And the information she provided me with, so far, was what I expected to hear. The perpetrator was an adult family member; she was nine when it happened; it involved genital touching ("He asked me to masturbate him"), digital penetration ("He would stick his fingers inside me"), and oral genital contact ("He would ask me to perform fellatio"); and it happened between five and ten times over a period of six months. Based on the objective characteristics of the abuse experiences (the who, what, and when), she fit the standard profile of an abuse victim to a tee. But the rest of the interview did not go so well.

I asked Erin to talk about the subjective characteristics of the abuse: what the sexual abuse was like for her when it was happening, how she reacted to it, how she felt about it, and what she did. It was in this part of the interview that I would be collecting the data at the heart of the study—data about how traumatic the abuse was for the victim. According to the interview protocol, I would begin by asking Erin to quantitatively rate, on a five-point scale, questions related to how traumatic the abuse was when it happened (five was very much so; one, not at all).

"Okay, can you rate how frightened you were?"

"Frightened?"

"Yes, frightened."

"Umm. You mean at the time of the abuse?"

"Yes, at the time of the abuse."

"Not very . . . maybe a two?"

"Can you rate how painful it was for you . . . on the same five-point scale?"

"Painful? Not at all. No, not painful. A one."

"Can you tell me how shocked you were?"

"Well, it was surprising at first, so maybe a three?"

"What about overwhelmed? Did you feel over-whelmed when it was happening?"

"Hmm. No, I would not say overwhelmed. A one and a half maybe?"

"Okay—so overall, how traumatic would you say the experience was when it happened?"

"Hmm . . . at the time it happened?"

"Yes."

"About a two."

Considering that Erin definitely met criteria as a sexual abuse victim, and considering my indoctrination into the theory that sexual abuse was invariably a traumatic experience for the child victim, I wondered how her ratings of trauma could be so low. I was supposed to stick to my standardized questions and not to deviate too much from the interview protocol. But what I was hearing just did not make sense. I figured I'd go off the interview and consider Erin to be a pilot subject who could help me make sure my interview questions made sense.

"Erin," I said. "You were sexually abused as a nine-year-old, multiple times, by someone you trusted. . . ."

Why wasn't it more traumatic for you when it was happening?"

She looked directly at me with her clear, icy-blue eyes. "Because I did not understand what was going on."

"What do you mean?" I said.

"What I mean is that I did not understand what sex was. I did not understand what he was asking me to do. I did not know why he would want me to do that, to touch him there, to put that in my mouth. I did not know anything, at all, about sexual matters. I supposed I had led a sheltered life. He said it was normal and I chose to believe him."

Okay, I thought to myself. But even if she did not understand exactly what was going on, surely she could tell it was wrong, right? That this should not be happening?

"I could tell by the way he was acting that this was something I wasn't supposed to talk about—and once the front door opened while we were doing it, he jumped up really fast so I could tell we were doing something wrong."

But if she knew it was wrong, why did she not stop it? Say no? Why did it happen so many times? I paused for a moment and then asked, "Why do you think you didn't tell anyone?"

For the first time she did not answer. She closed her eyes, put her long fingers on her forehead, and began massaging her eyebrows. After a while she leaned down and began fishing in her big leather purse.

"Do you need something?" I asked.

"No," she said. "I'm fine. Totally fine."

I could not see her face, but I could hear some muffled sniffles. I reached across and handed her the Kleenex box on my desk. After she wiped her eyes and blew her nose and made a brief visit to the ladies room, she seemed different—less distant, more relaxed. She ate a donut.

"Look, it's complicated. I knew him. He was part of the family. . . . If it was a stranger, I guess I would have said no, just run away. But it was not a stranger. I loved him. I trusted him. It did not occur to me that he would want to do something like that. . . . On top of it, he was an adult, and I was always being told to listen to adults, to do what they ask. . . . I didn't want to say no, to say no to something he would ask. And why would I be defying him? I couldn't even explain it. . . . It did not occur to me that he would do something to harm me. . . . I made a decision. I did a kind of cost-benefit analysis, although I could not of course have understood it in those terms. What would happen, the cost of saying yes? I was not sure, maybe get into some kind of trouble? Cost of saying no—having to defy him or stand up to an adult. That would have been difficult to do. And the benefits? If I did it—this thing I didn't really understand—I would be making him happy. . . . Whatever it was clearly it was something that he wanted. . . . I wanted to do what he wanted. . . . I guess you could say I was eager to please."

As a nine-year-old, Erin faced a complicated decision, one in which, from her perspective as a child, there was no clearly correct choice. In the absence of necessary information (for example, what sex was and why his behavior was wrong, what the long-term consequences might be for her or for him if anyone found out), she made the best choice she could.

At the end of the interview, Erin said she was glad she made time to come in, that it felt cathartic to talk about the sexual abuse and "finally get it off her chest." I felt differently. Nothing went as I had expected. What Erin told me made no sense. It was a terrible experience for me even to hear about the details of her abuse—shocking, revolting, heartbreaking—so why was it not more terrible for her when it actually happened?

At first I assumed that Erin was an unusual victim—
that I had picked the wrong subject to be my first interview. This turned out not to be the case.

• • •

SAMUEL WAS A SIX-FOOT-PLUS, extremely attractive,
African American policeman. In his late forties and divorced with adult children, he was the next participant
in my study.

Like Erin, Samuel clearly met criteria for sexual
abuse.

> I went to this bible camp as a kid. . . . In the
> neighborhood I come from, there was not much
> to do in the summer except for get in trouble so
> my mother sent me there. I was maybe nine or
> ten. . . . They didn't like for us to go to the bath-
> room alone so usually one of the counselors
> would go with you. He was maybe in his twen-
> ties. His name was John and we thought he was
> pretty cool with us kids, so we liked him more
> than the other ones. I had to pee but I didn't
> want to pee in front of him so I went into the
> stall. When I came out he said he had to check
> me to make sure I had cleaned myself properly.

I didn't know what he was talking about but he told me to take down my pants and show him. . . . He said that it wasn't clean, that I had made a mess on myself, and he said he was going to clean it with his mouth. . . . Then he said that he had to go to the bathroom and then I had to check if he was clean . . . I had to put it in my mouth to check. . . . He made me keep it in his mouth for a while. I don't think he came—ejaculated if you know what I mean—but I am not sure. He did this a number of times over the rest of the summer. Sometimes I had to clean him with a tissue and my hand, sometimes in my mouth.

Based on the objective characteristics, Samuel was a "normal" sexual abuse victim. He was abused by someone he knew, the abuse involved oral sex, and he was about ten. But again, when it came to the part of the interview when we discussed the subjective characteristics of the abuse, I was in for a surprise. Samuel, like Erin, did not report that the abuse, when it happened, was particularly traumatic.

"Did it hurt?"

"Oh, no. No, I would not say it hurt."

"Were you scared?"

"No, not at all. Maybe a little weirded out. . . . Confused is a better word."

"Where you shocked or horrified?"

"No, that's too strong to put it. Maybe surprised?"

"Can you tell me what the abuse was like for you when it happened?"

"I would say . . . complicated. Let's see. . . . It is hard to explain. . . . I guess to be totally honest, I didn't really understand what was going on. I was a pretty innocent kid. . . . I didn't actually know what a blow job was. . . . Actually, what was going through my mind is why would he want me to kiss him [there]."

"So are you saying that you did not understand what was going on? You didn't understand that it was sexual in nature?"

"I didn't understand. . . . I mean, if I had to tell someone I would not be able to describe what it was we were doing. . . . I could kind of sense it was wrong—by the way he was reacting—like trying to be quiet and telling me we shouldn't talk about it. . . . Also, it didn't hurt or anything. . . . So there were no bells going off, no alarms going whoop whoop whoop this is wrong."

• • •

SOON AFTER MY MEETING WITH SAMUEL, I saw Carole, a forty-six-year-old homemaker. Her three kids played in the kitchen area at the entrance of the lab while I interviewed her.

> When I was six my father died and we moved to my . . . grandparents' home. They lived in an old farmhouse in Connecticut. . . . I was pretty lonely there. . . . We used to live in a city. . . . Now I was on this five-acre farm in the middle of nowhere but I loved my grandparents. I did; I was close to them. . . . My mother was very close to her mother. They were always together, but my grandfather and I, we were . . . inseparable. . . . At the time he was like my best friend—my only close friend. . . . We lived there for about two years and I spent a lot of time with my grandfather and he wasn't that well—he couldn't get around too good, so a lot of the time . . . he spent in the TV room that was off the porch. . . . Well, here comes the hard part. . . . Sometimes when I was watching TV I'd sit on his lap . . . and sometimes when I was on his lap he would put his hands on me . . . up my skirt . . . under my underwear . . . and, well, he'd feel me . . . my

vagina area. . . . It was maybe off and on for a year or so. . . . Sometimes he would push himself up against me, rub my crotch against his and he would be breathing really hard. . . . Sometimes I would feel wetness; my panties would be sticky.

Carole was a little younger than most victims but certainly well within the common age range. Like Erin and Samuel, from an objective perspective, she was clearly abused—an adult engaged in sexual activities with her when she was young. But from a subjective perspective, as a child, she did not see it as abuse. She trusted the perpetrator, and what he was doing did not hurt. She had no idea what sex was. While she could sense it was wrong, she was not quite sure. She figured the best course of action was just to go along with what was being done to her.

"I'll tell you, I didn't like it, what he was doing, but I just didn't really understand. . . . I guess I just thought of it as something we did on Grandpa's lap when we watched TV."

• • •

THESE INITIAL PARTICIPANTS' stories ended up being remarkably consistent with what other victims who participated told me over the following years. In fact, less than 10 percent of the participants reported experiencing their abuse as traumatic, terrifying, overwhelming, life-threatening, or shocking at the time it happened.

And why was it not traumatic? Usually the perpetrator was someone they knew, admired, loved, and trusted—not, as one victim put it, "a freak wearing a hockey mask and carrying a knife." In addition, what this person asked them to do did not hurt—it almost always involved touching or kissing of the genitals—and it was not accompanied by force or aggression.

As Kristin, a twenty-seven-year-old architecture student, described it, "One night I woke up and he [her new stepfather] was kneeling next to my bed. He said he liked to watch me sleep. He told me I was beautiful. That it was nice to see me sleeping so peacefully. Stuff like that. Then I think what happened the first time is that he took my hand and put it on him. On his penis. He moved it up and down and then after a while he was breathing heavy and then I felt some wetness on my hand. Then he told me that I was such a good girl, that I made him feel good."

Tom, a high school guidance counselor, said, "There was nothing violent about it; there was nothing coerced with threat, you know, like 'I'll kill you' or 'I'll tell your

parents' or something like that. It was all verrrrry subtle. And subtle in the sense that I didn't even know it
was wrong."

Initially, from my perspective as a researcher and
academic, it did not matter that they knew, liked, or
trusted the perpetrator. It did not matter that no force
or aggression was used. The experiences were still horrible, and listening to the details filled me with fear,
shock, and revulsion. As an adult I understood that the
events occurring were sexual in nature, very wrong,
and an egregious violation of a child's rights. But I was
forced to confront, over and over again, the perspective
of the child being abused. I had to get out of my own
head and into theirs (as children) and see that their reactions to these experiences were different. Victims
said that since they did not understand what the perpetrator was doing or asking them to do, they had no way
to process or make sense of sexually toned encounters.
The word used by 92 percent of the victims when
asked to describe how they were feeling? Confusion.
Some randomly sampled victims in my study described
the experience as follows:

It was weird; I had no way to describe it.

He had his pants down; I think he had no under-
wear on. It just didn't make any sense to me.

It didn't hurt me, and I was too young to think
of it as sexual. . . . The experience just did not
fit into my notions of right and wrong.

Although they were confused, most of the victims
who spoke with me (about 85 percent) said that they
could sense that something about the situation was
wrong. Again, some of the victims who spoke with me
described it as follows:

I knew it wasn't right for him to have fingers up
underneath my panties. . . . I knew in my little
mind it was wrong.

Oh, I knew there was something wrong, but I
just didn't know what to call it really.

At some point he said I shouldn't tell anyone because this was something special between him
and me and that it was very normal. I believed
him. It didn't feel normal, but it didn't feel bad

either. Basically when it was happening I had no
idea what was going on.

Many of the victims said they sensed that what was
happening was wrong because of the way the perpetrator was acting. They told me,

> I only knew it was wrong because he told me
> not to tell my mother and he would be real
> quiet; he'd tell me not to make any noise.

> By the way he was acting, I could kind of figure
> out that it was something we weren't supposed
> to be doing.

Everything I knew dictated that the abuse should be a
horrible experience, that the child should be traumatized at the time it was happening—overwhelmed with
fear, shock, and horror. But the sexual abuse described
by the victims I spoke with was much different. It was
not a black-and-white situation. It was complicated,
subtle. A trusted person had asked each of these children to do something he or she did not fully understand. Although they could often sense it was wrong,
they were not sure why.

So what did they do? In stark contrast to everything I had come to believe about sexual abuse, they did
not fight it. It was not done against their will. They
went along—did what was asked of them. In their own
words, they "participated," "consented," and "allowed
it." In fact, of those who sensed the behavior was wrong,
only 5 percent tried to stop it—by saying no, running
away, or telling a parent. Why? The trauma theory
holds that a child will only participate in abuse if
forced, threatened, or explicitly coerced. This was true
in a very small minority of cases. Most of the victims I
spoke with had very different motivations. According
to them, they did not resist the abuse for three reasons.

First of all, they told me that when they were children, adults often asked them to do things they did not
really understand or want to do. Accepting confusing,
unpleasant things is, for better or worse, an inevitable
part of life as a child. As Dave, an accountant, put it, "I
would say I had no idea what was going on. What he
was doing just made no sense. . . . But I think as a kid
so much of what happens to you is weird and confusing
that this just sort of joined the ranks with the rest of
the stuff. . . . Basically I was the sort of kid who just
learned to accept what they are told by adults and not
complain much." In the words of Maria, a mother of

two teenagers who was undergoing treatment for breast cancer, "He was my doctor and it seemed like every time I had to see him he did things that were weird and sort of hurt. Let me just say that this hurt much less than the shot he gave me on my shoulder. That had about a million needles sticking out of it."

Second, not only are kids routinely asked to do things they do not understand or like, but they are told to listen to adults—especially adults in positions of authority. As Bob, a construction worker, put it, "I was brought up in the kind of family that you listen to adults. You do what they say and you don't ask too many questions." "It never occurred to me to say no to anything a teacher asked me to do," noted Joy, a therapist. In the words of Robert, an attorney specializing in medical malpractice, "He was a priest. You listen to priests. I told my father I didn't want to go, that I didn't want to spend time with him and he [said,] 'Just shut up. . . . Be happy such a person even wants to give you attention.'"

Resisting the abuse would require children to challenge authority, something they are told not to do. Many reported being very concerned about the negative consequences of saying no to the perpetrator:

He might be upset with me. I didn't want that.

I didn't want to hurt his feelings. He was really nice most of the time.

I don't know why, I can't explain it, but it would be totally embarrassing to say no . . . and not really to have a reason why I was saying no to this person.

It didn't exactly feel normal, but there was no way I was going to say no. He was my teacher. I didn't want to end up getting sent to the principal's office for disrespect.

In short, these victims felt they could resist, but doing so would require questioning authority, and they did not feel comfortable with that, especially when they could not clearly articulate why they would be resisting.

Now add this third factor to further complicate matters: The abusers often conferred "rewards" on their victims for saying yes. These ranged from concrete rewards like gifts ("He took me to Penny's and would buy me something afterwards," "I liked ice cream a lot and he gave me ice cream") to abstract but powerful reinforcements like love and attention ("He told me I would [do it] if I loved him and I wanted him to know I loved him," "As a kid I never got much attention and at least this was attention," "Back then I was looking for any kind of love or approval I could get," "I remember thinking this person would like me more if I did it. . . . I wanted so much for him to like me, to want to be around me"). Although I did not specifically ask victims about dysfunctional family backgrounds or childhood neglect, many reported often being left alone as children: "Both of my parents were busy," or "I came from single-parent home. My dad left and my mom had to work hard to make the ends meet. I hardly ever saw her." More than a few volunteered that they felt neglected as children: "I could sense it was wrong, but the thing is I think I needed some attention," or "I was so lonely a lot of the time, didn't have brothers and sisters . . . and he, well, I guess you could say was around for me . . . took me places, bought me things."

Some subjects—in no cases victims of penetration—reported that they responded sexually to what happened to them, that sometimes it felt good ("I didn't understand it, but I guess my body did"; "It was confusing, but I liked it. It felt good"; "It was the first context in which I had sexual pleasure"). One subject, who was sexually victimized by his camp counselor, was quite

clear that, at the time, he enjoyed it: "I used to look forward to him sneaking into my bunk. It felt good. What
he was doing felt good. It was the first time I developed
erections. When he stopped . . . I thought he was doing it
to someone else. . . . I was mad at him." Another man told
me that during his abuse (by a priest), he had his first
orgasm: "I was, what, maybe twelve? I had no idea what
was going on. . . . I knew it was wrong, but I also knew it
felt good. Totally fucked up, if you know what I mean."

Sometimes, heartbreakingly, the benefits extended
to a better life for the victim, as in the case of a man
(one of the 5 percent of victims whose abuse involved
intercourse) who told me, "Well sometimes it hurt, but
it was a hell of a lot better than having to go back to
social services." Even worse, for some victims the better life extended to others:

> He made my mom happy and I didn't want to
> interfere with that.

> He paid the bills, bought us a car. . . . Whatever
> it was it seemed like a small price to pay in return.

In short, even though many victims sensed that what
was happening was wrong, they found it very difficult to

say no. Considering the abuse from their perspective, this began to make sense to me. They were not quite sure why it was wrong. The perpetrator was someone they had been told to listen to. On top of all that, the victims often benefited from saying yes. It was an extremely complicated situation for these children—one, from their perspective, with no clearly correct choice. So they made the best choice they could: They consented. And we cannot fault them for making this choice. Considering that they faced confusing circumstances armed with inadequate information, it was actually quite rational.[1]

As I learned more, I felt a growing sense of anxiety. With support from research grants and from my advisors in the psychology department, I had invested a lot of time, energy, and money into this project. But clearly I must have done something wrong. Despite my best efforts, I must have found a very unusual group of sexual abuse victims.

Right?

2

The Truth About
Sexual Abuse

HARVARD UNIVERSITY and affiliated institutions (Harvard Medical School, Cambridge Hospital, McLean Hospital) are well known worldwide as centers for trauma research. It is not difficult to find people to discuss your findings with, and psychologists, psychiatrists, clinical social workers, and graduate students were more than willing to give me their input when I came to them with my results.

Their most common reaction? Precisely what I suspected: There must be something unusual about the victims. I must have a sampling problem.

What kind of problem specifically? Perhaps the victims who responded to my ad, agreed to participate, and showed up for the interview had experienced less severe abuse compared to most victims in the population. According to a clinical psychologist who treated patients at Cambridge Hospital's Victims of Violence Program (one of the nation's preeminent treatment programs for adult victims of childhood sexual abuse), if I looked at the objective characteristics of what happened to my victims, I might find that those who participated in my study had experienced, in her own words, more "benign" abuse compared to most other victims in the general population.

To determine whether the victims who participated in my research study experienced more benign abuse than most, I needed to track down all the national probability studies that existed on the objective characteristics of sexual abuse. According to all of them, I had to disagree with the clinical psychologist who specialized in treating victims of sexual abuse. There was nothing particularly benign or unusual about the abuse the subjects who participated in my study had endured. In terms of the objective characteristics of the abuse, their experiences mirrored those of the general population of people who are sexually abused. Abusers are almost always someone the children and their families know, the type of abuse reported usually involves kissing and genital touching, force or violence is rarely involved, and injuries (minor or severe) occur in less than 10 percent of cases. What happened to the victims in my research study was remarkably consistent with national sample studies of victims in the United States.[1]

• • •

PLAYING DEVIL'S ADVOCATE, I supposed I could see why a therapist who specialized in treating victims of sexual abuse who seek therapy would assume that the victims participating in my study had experienced abuse that was relatively benign. Some research shows that, on average, victims who seek treatment (or who are referred to treatment) report abuse more severe than the norm (for example, the abuse more likely involved force or violence or required medical attention).[2] Thus, reversing this psychologist's explanation, I realized that it was probably the victims she saw in the office who reported unusual abuse, not the people participating in my research study.

The head of Cambridge Hospital's psychiatry department at the time had another explanation for me. If there was nothing unusual about the abuse the people I interviewed experienced, then perhaps something unusual about the victims as children caused them not to be traumatized. Were they younger or older than most victims? Based on national studies, the average age of sexual abuse is about ten, with most of the abuse occurring before age twelve and about one-third occurring before age nine. This was true of my sample. He then suggested that maybe I had managed to find a particularly resilient sample of victims, people who for whatever reason were "tougher" or "less sensitive" to disturbing social interactions than most victims. This explanation made no sense. How resilient could they be? Almost every single one of them reported that these experiences had damaged them: symptoms of post-traumatic stress disorder (PTSD), major depression, drug and alcohol abuse, and sexual problems (ranging from lack of interest to inability to orgasm to hypersexuality) were extremely common. Of my sample, 75 percent reported self-esteem problems; 50 percent reported feeling cut off from others or alienated because of the abuse; and almost 90 percent reported difficulties in relationships. Many victims said the abuse had multiple negative aftereffects. Comments like this were common:

> It created a whole bunch of issues for me surrounding trust, intimacy, control and food, and other people. It's affected all my life. There's nothing untouched.

What happened to me changed me. It affected how well I can trust other people . . . how I feel about myself and my self-esteem. There is a level of shame . . . how can I put it? Self-loathing? That is always there after all these years. I can't think of any area of my life that has not been damaged.

These victims had been affected in the same way as most others reported being damaged. They were not particularly resilient. In fact, any rational person in the field would assume that the abuse must have been very traumatic when it happened. It was simply my asking about that dimension of the experience that revealed that it hadn't necessarily been so.

The next set of explanations for my data were directed less at the subjects who participated in the study and more at me. Were the diagnostic interviews and questionnaires I used to assess psychological damage—for example, the existence of disorders such as depression and PTSD—valid? Yes, they were. I used only instruments widely accepted in the field.[3] Was I properly trained in diagnostic interviewing? Yes, I was. I had been trained by experts at the National Institute of Mental Health and passed my diagnostic training classes at Harvard with no problems at all. Were the questions I used to assess how traumatic the sexual abuse was when it happened misleading or biased? According to my advisor and colleagues at Harvard, they were not. In the event that we were all out of touch with reality, I consulted the CEO of a large, global-marketing research company that did polling for outlets like *Time* magazine about whether the questions made sense. He deemed them clear and straightforward.

At a brown-bag departmental lunch where gradu-ate students, faculty, and researchers got together to discuss their data, another explanation emerged. Many of the lunch participants came from the field of cogni-tive psychology and specialized in memory functioning. Perhaps victims were not reporting their abuse as trau-matic because they were not remembering it correctly. Perhaps the retrospective nature of the study rendered it vulnerable to inaccurate recollections.

This was possible, I reasoned. As the head of Har-vard's Department of Psychology explains in his beau-tifully written book *Searching for Memory*, our memory systems are quite fallible. Memories are subject to decay and distortion over time.[4] The details of early child-hood experiences can be difficult to remember correctly, and most of the victims in the study were recalling events that had happened decades before.[5]

But there were problems with this explanation. Experts in the field had specifically advised me to collect data on populations of adults. Why? Because kids rarely report abuse (more on this later), and those who do often experience abuse severer than the norm. Further, I had no proof the victims were remembering incorrectly. Neither did anyone else. In addition, retrospective research is the most common type of research done in the trauma field. In fact, the diagnosis of posttraumatic stress disorder is based on patients' memories of past experiences.[6] If my data were going to be explained away as subject to inaccurate memory recall, then trauma professionals would have to explain away most of the research conducted in the field. Finally, even if this inaccurate memory theory was correct and my victims were misremembering what had happened, they should be remembering it as more traumatic than it actually was. Research shows that people have a tendency to let current psychological states bias their memories of past events. The worse you feel at the time someone asks you about a previous event in your life, the worse you remember the past event to be.[7] If the people I interviewed were psychologically distressed at the time I spoke with them (which they definitely were), one might expect them to, if anything, remember the abuse as worse than it actually was.

Increasingly eager to understand my data, I invited an internationally recognized expert on psychological trauma[8] to give a talk as part of a series on PTSD that I was organizing for postdoctoral research fellows at Harvard Medical School. I asked him my million-dollar question: Why are my sexual abuse victims not remembering their experience as traumatic? Seemingly unfazed by the question, he answered without skipping a beat. It had to do with dissociation, a theoretical defense mechanism of the mind (similar to repression) that kicks in to help victims mute or escape the psychological and physical pain they are experiencing. In plain English, as a consequence of dissociation, victims "space out," their minds "drift out of their bodies," they lull themselves into a sort of "minitrance"—all ways to distance themselves from the reality of the situation they are confronting.[9] In short, according to this trauma expert, the victims who spoke to me did not report any trauma because the abuse was so traumatic that they had dissociated when it was happening and as a consequence could not remember it correctly.

Others in the audience nodded solemnly as he explained his conclusions; they seemed satisfied with this explanation. But I did not feel the same way. In fact, I felt a little sick. Maybe he and other scholars who endorsed this theory were right. Perhaps sexual abuse was so traumatic when it happened that victims dissociated and thus "forgot" the pain. The theory sounded intriguing (it was exactly the kind of theory that made me want to be a psychologist in the first place), but the victims had a different explanation, a simpler one. They made it very clear to me that the abuse was not traumatic for them when it was happening because they had not understood what was going on.

· · ·

THERE IS A FUNDAMENTAL PRINCIPLE of science referred to as Occam's razor. When deciding between two competing explanations for data, you should choose the simpler, more parsimonious one. The idea is that there can be any number of explanations for phenomena you are trying to understand, so when confronted with multiple competing hypotheses, select the one that introduces the fewest assumptions and postulates the fewest entities. In other words, all things being equal, the simplest solution is usually the best.[10] Given the choice between a complicated, theoretical, unconscious defense mechanism and victims' explanations, according to Occam's razor, I should listen to the victims. They said they did not understand what was happening to them. And if they did not get it, on what basis would they be traumatized? On what basis would they dissociate or repress feelings of terror? Where would the feeling of terror be coming from?

What's more, science, as I had been taught, is about developing theories that can be falsified; hypothetically, data could emerge that would actually disprove them.[11] Yet, it seemed the assumption that sexual abuse is traumatic was itself "unfalsifiable." Anything a victim said that ran counter to the trauma theory professionals in the trauma field reinterpreted to support it instead. The theory could not be proven wrong. It appeared victims could say nothing that would make experts believe them.

• • •

ON THE TRAIN COMING HOME from the panel on PTSD, I finally realized that there might not be anything wrong with me or my research methods and that I was correct to believe what the victims who participated in my research study remembered and told me.

I did not question that sexual abuse is related to adult psychological damage. Thirty years of solid research indicated that this was the case. Nor did I question that traumatic experiences, in general, could cause long-term psychological damage. There was neurobiological research to support this as well. I did question, however, whether sexual abuse was usually a traumatic experience when it happened. I needed to go back to the books. This time, rather than focusing exclusively on what experts had to say, it was time to focus on what victims had to say. What was sexual abuse usually like when it happened?

Given the wide acceptance of the trauma assumption about sexual abuse, one might suppose that thousands of studies had asked victims this question. I discovered that this is not the case. As one researcher puts it, "The systematic exploration of the subjective experience of minors involved in sexual contact with adults, contacts of either positive or negative quality, has generally been absent from the literature."[12] After weeks on Medline and Psychinfo (the two most widely used databases in the fields of psychiatry and psychology), I found approximately twenty published studies conducted within the last one hundred years that asked victims specifically to describe what their abuse was like when it happened.

In his 1938 study of married women, the cognitive psychologist Lewis Terman asked if respondents had had a sexual experience before age fifteen that shocked or greatly disgusted them, and 32 percent said yes. In another sample of married women, 24.6 reported "sex shock."[13] In Alfred Kinsey's seminal study published in *Sexual Behavior in the Human Female* in 1953, he reported that 80 percent of his sample said they had been emotionally upset or frightened by their contact with adults.[14] In 1956, Judson Landis presented data from seventy-three children of "sex deviates" referred to a clinic in San Francisco for treatment; 33 percent of girls were frightened at the time of the abuse, 26 percent of boys.[15] In 1991 Paul Okami, one of the few researchers who asked victims specific questions about how they felt at the time of the abuse, found that many victims reported ambivalent responses. For example, reactions ranged from fear to confusion and shame to interest and excitement, and often the same victim reported multiple emotions simultaneously. Among those who rated the experience as 100 percent negative (about 40 percent of Okami's sample), force or violence was present in only 14.3 percent of these cases. Further, the most common reasons endorsed for why the experience was negative had nothing to do with fear or shock but resulted from the fact that "something was done to me that I didn't like or didn't understand" or "the experience confused me and made me anxious because I couldn't tell if it was right or wrong."[16] In a 1983 study of victims surveyed in a college sample in West Virginia, about 15 percent reported fear.[17] In a 1999 national sample study, 30 percent of victims reported that the abuse was frightening when it happened.[18] In 2006 a team of researchers out of Holland's University of Maastricht asked sexual abuse victims who had "recovered" memories of their sexual abuse to retrospectively rate the emotions they felt during their abuse experiences. Some 85 percent of their sample "failed to appreciate their abuse as traumatic at the time it occurred."[19]

Rather than asking victims to rate aspects of trauma, many studies had them classify their abuse experiences based on broad categories such as predominately positive (usually consisting of words such as "pleasant," "sexy," and "exciting"), predominantly negative (consisting of words such as "shameful," "frightening," "shocking," and "embarrassing"), or neutral. To note some of these studies here, psychologist Carney Landis found that 56 percent of victims in his sample considered the abuse unpleasant or extremely unpleasant, but "only in rare cases was it traumatic."[20] In 1965, John

Gagnon reanalyzed data from Kinsey's original study and found that victims could be classified into two categories: those who found the experience to be mostly negative and those who found it to be mostly neutral or positive. The majority reported that they reacted negatively to the abuse.[21] In David Finkelhor's widely cited study of sexual abuse victims in Boston, victims rated their experience on a five-point scale (from positive to negative). The average rating was a three. He concluded that "contrary to the stereotype, most victims readily acknowledge the positive as well as the negative elements of their experience."[22] In Diane Russell's seminal book *The Secret Trauma*, women in San Francisco rated their abuse experiences on a five-point scale in terms of how "upset" they had been: 33 percent of the sample reported being extremely upset.[23] In another retrospective survey, researchers reported that the most common reaction at the time of the abuse was "unpleasant confusion" and "embarrassment."[24]

While the methodology of these studies differed wildly in terms of the questions asked and how the data were analyzed, the takeaway is fairly consistent. Sexual abuse, for many victims, is not a traumatic experience when it happens. While most report sexual abuse as a negative experience, the word "negative" is simply not synonymous with terror, horror, fear, or pain. As clinical psychologist Eve Carlson reminds researchers, to be classified as traumatic, an abuse experience either has to involve the threat of death, serous injury, or harm or at least produce the kind of overwhelming fear and helplessness responses that such threats do.[25]

Indeed, further to the research I've highlighted above, David Finkelhor, the director of the tremendously influential Center for Child Victimization and a well-known sexual abuse researcher at the University of New Hampshire, states,

The conceptualization that has won the most support is the idea that the impact of sexual abuse constitutes a form of posttraumatic stress disorder . . . but the theory behind PTSD does not readily adapt to the experience of sexual abuse. The classic PTSD theory says the symptoms result from "an overwhelming event resulting in helplessness in the face of intolerable danger: anxiety and instinctual arousal. . . . This theory is well suited to traumas such a war shock and rape and probably to sexual abuse that occurs under violent circumstances. However, much sexual abuse does not occur under

conditions of danger, threat and violence. . . .
Abuse experiences may be degrading, humiliat-
ing and stigmatizing but not necessarily frightening or threatening to bodily integrity. . . .
Sexual abuse cannot be subsumed or explained
within the framework of Post Traumatic Stress
Disorder."[26]

Margaret Hagan, a professor at Boston University,
concurs: "The absence of clear trauma, violence or
threat and fear in so many cases should prohibit the im-
position of the trauma model in cases where it does not
fit." She goes on to note, "That the research leads to no
does not, however, lead researchers to accept no as an
answer to questions about the validity of the trauma
model."[27]

Indeed, many professionals interested in sexual
abuse are quick to explain away what the victims in
studies have to say. In *The Secret Trauma*, Diane Russell
explains why so few of her victims report trauma similarly to Bessel van der Kolk, by endorsing defenses of
denial, dissociation, and repression.[28] Others simply ignore what victims have to say. In one of the most
widely cited papers in the sexual abuse field, Kathleen
Kendall-Tacket and her colleagues at the University of

New Hampshire's influential Family Research Center, after reviewing the overall results of forty-five studies that do not support trauma as a useful model for most cases of child abuse, nevertheless stress that the study of sexual abuse victims "has important relevance to other theory and research concerning how children process trauma . . . how trauma expresses itself at various developmental stages, [and] its role in the development of later pathology."[29] Today, experts either implicitly or explicitly rely on stress and trauma models. The logical failure of these models appears entirely irrelevant to the strength with which they continue to be held.

• • •

WHAT I DISCOVERED as I explored this body of research reassured me. But considering all the evidence that existed indicating that sexual abuse was not a traumatic experience, why is the trauma model so dominant, so entrenched in the study of this sexual crime?

One explanation comes from the field of child development, specifically from researchers who study how average children understand and react to sexual information. Such researchers believe that professionals in the sexual abuse field suffer from an adultcentric

bias; they try to understand sexual abuse experiences using an adult framework rather than a child-generated
framework. In their excellent book *Treatment and Prevention of Childhood Sexual Abuse: A Child-Generated Model*,
child clinical psychologists Sandra Burkhardt and Anthony Rotatori elaborate on this idea: "Due to the
morally reprehensible nature of child sexual abuse, researchers have an understandable tendency to project
their adult fears, repulsion and horror onto child victims,
to assume they react like they do when faced with sexual
situations." Their anger is barely contained: "Amid the
adult posturing, children's views are seldom heard," and
other researchers agree.[30] In a controversial chapter titled "The Professional Response to Child Sexual Abuse,"
the authors, all respected professionals in the sexual
abuse field, conclude, "It is amazing that well-meaning
professionals acting in children's interests have chosen
to all but ignore children's experience of these actions."[31]

As philosophers of science have written, although
scientists are supposed to base their theories on data,
this is not always easy to do. We all tend to be deduc-
tivists, not inductivists, in our approach to the world.
We do not simply gather data and draw raw, unbiased
conclusions; rather, we have prior information and
theories that guide data gathering and interpretation.

Karl Popper clarifies this position: "The belief that we can start with pure observations alone, without anything in the nature of a theory, is absurd. . . . Observation is always selective. . . . For the animal a point of view is provided by its needs, the tasks of the moment and its expectations; for the scientist by his theoretical interest, the special problem under investigation, his conjectures and anticipations and the theories which he accepts as a kind of background; his frame of reference, his horizon of expectations."[32]

Sexual abuse is what psychologist Steven Pinker calls a "dangerous topic"—one that arouses painful and intense emotions in people who are forced to think about it. In the grip of such emotions, it is difficult for many people (even trained scientists) to think clearly.[33] Our "horizon of expectations" is likely subject to strong influence by the moral and even psychological revulsion many of us feel when we think about adults using innocent children for sexual purposes. We project these feelings onto the victims and assume they see the world in the same way.

As the field of child cognition shows us, beginning at least with Jean Piaget in the mid-twentieth century, this is unfair to the child. Children do not think and reason like adults; rather, their thinking and reasoning about themselves, other people, and the world around them unfold over time and through experience.[34] When it comes to sex, they do not understand the full meaning of sexual activities and behavior until late in childhood, usually just prior to the early stages of adolescence. Until then, children have only a dim sense of adult sexuality. Due to their age and level of development, they are cognitively unable to grasp the meaning of sexual encounters. They cannot understand sex or sexually toned encounters like adults can.[35] As David Finkelhor puts it, "What may seem like a horrible violation of social taboos from an adult perspective need not be so to a child. A sexual experience with an adult may be something unusual, vaguely unpleasant, even traumatic at the moment, but not a horror story."[36] In short, because children have a very amorphous idea about what is sexual, they are likely not to recognize sexual action and intention on the part of others or to interpret them as something else. Jon Conte and Lucy Berliner, an expert in sexual abuse working out of the Sexual Assault Center at Seattle's Harborview Medical Center, clearly support this point. In a paper titled "The Process of Victimization: The Victims' Perspective," they note that the majority of sexual abuse victims they studied did not know they were being sexually abused at the time the abuse was happening. No differently from the subjects who spoke with me, the victims made such statements as "I didn't know there was anything wrong with it, because I didn't know it was abuse until later. I thought he was showing me affection."[37]

A few years ago, researchers at a prominent Seattle clinic for sexual abuse victims interviewed children whose abuse had come to the attention of mental health officials (and therefore was more likely to represent extreme cases). They asked these children to describe what had happened in their own words. Their heartbreaking responses confirm what I have explored above. Kids do not get it. Here are some of their comments:

> He had a tail. . . . It grew. . . . He tried to put it in me.

> My brother does bad things. . . . He does naughty things to me. . . . He does something but I don't know what it is [child points at her vagina].

> My brother stuck his tail in my bottom and he asked me to suck on it. It's supposed to be a secret. I don't like how it tastes, but I didn't want my brother mad at me.[38]

As I discussed earlier, although child victims often exhibit a lack of knowledge about the exact nature of the experiences they are confronted with, many can sense that they are wrong. Here is how Ross Cheit, a Brown University professor who was sexually abused in the late 1960s, described it: "The concept of trauma never felt right to me. It never fit my story. . . . There were no threats. I never sensed danger. I didn't fear him. He was nice to me. Something didn't add up—and it slowly started bothering me more and more. . . . I knew I had been 'had,' so to speak, but I couldn't understand it."[39]

Twenty years ago, Leda Cosmides was one of the first to postulate that humans have a naturally evolved mental mechanism devoted to detecting cheaters, a kind of built-in way to detect when people are lying to or betraying us. According to her theory, the ability to reason rapidly and accurately about social contracts may have conferred some evolutionary advantage to our species; it was important for survival and reproductive fitness.[40] Subsequent research not only supports the idea that such an evolutionary adaptive cheating detector exists in humans but suggests that we show evidence of it early on in life. As anyone who has spent much time with a young child can attest, the cry of "That's not fair!" is often heard and is quite accurate. As a species, we appear to be highly attuned to betrayals, even when we cannot define them exactly. A child can often sense that abuse is wrong because the perpetrator communicates in some way that what is happening is bad (by warning the child not to tell anyone, making sure the abuse is done covertly, or reacting with fear if anyone sees them together).

Children's knowledge of sex is a function of their level of cognitive development. If we can accept that, then we should be able to accept that their behavior is as well. Initially, I was shocked at how often victims told me that they participated in the abuse, that they went along with it, and that they did not fight it or report it. But the historical literature clearly delved into this phenomenon in great detail.

As far back as 1907, Karl Abraham noted that sexual abuse victims seem to fall into two separate categories. The first group he labeled "accidental victims." The abuse is violent, it is usually conducted by a stranger, and the victim is clearly aware that it is wrong. He or she reacts strongly and negatively to the offense and promptly reports it. Today, rather than "accidental" I might label this kind of abuse as "traumatic."

The second group Abraham labeled "participant victims." In this category, the abuse is not violent, and the victim knows the perpetrator, does not understand what is happening, often has more than one experience with the abuser, keeps the abuse a secret, and sometimes receives some reward from the offender.[41] Based on a review of the research, the participant victim is, by far, the more common type.[42] In 1977 Judith Herman and Linda Hirschman published a clinical study of fifteen adult women molested by their fathers as children. While the authors were 100 percent clear that the experiences were wrong, damaging, and criminal in nature, they were also quite clear that while "most of the study participants endured the sexual contact," in exchange "they received special treatment from the father and a sense of power and gratification in displacing the mother." The authors theorized that the fact that such experiences occurred was a function of "emotional deprivation" in the victims' histories.[43]

According to experts in child cognition, it should not be surprising that young people "allow" abuse. Not only do children not understand the full meaning or consequences of their actions, but they are conditioned biologically and psychologically to want and need very basic things: love, attention, positive feedback, and rewards. And this is precisely what perpetrators are offering them.[44] As Lucy Berliner eloquently notes, "A common method of coercion used by perpetrators involves the exploitation of child's normal need to feel loved, valued and cared for by parents. Children who do not have these needs met may be susceptible to the interest shown them by sexual offenders."[45] As one of the victims she studied put it, "I think it happened because I was so needy, because I didn't have anything."[46]

Consider Maya Angelou's description of her own account with sexual abuse in *I Know Why the Caged Bird Sings*. With heartbreaking honesty, she describes her childhood longing for affection, which led her to seek the attention of her mother's boyfriend. "I began to feel lonely for Mr. Freeman and the encasement of his big arms. Before, my world had been Bailey, food, Momma, the store, reading books and Uncle Willie. Now, for the first time it included physical contact."

Mr. Freeman took advantage of her attention. "I went over to him and sat quickly on his lap. At first, Mr. Freeman sat still, not holding me or anything, then I felt a soft lump under my thigh begin to move. It twitched against me and started to harden. Then he pulled me to his chest. . . . All the time he pushed me around on his lap, then suddenly he stood up and I slipped down to the floor. He ran to the bathroom." She clearly portrays the immense gulf in intention and understanding between adult and child: "He smelled of cola dust and grease and he was so close I buried my face in his shirt and listened to his heart, it was beating just for me..."[47]

Children comply, and to expect them to do otherwise is simply unrealistic.

Way back in 1956, Judson Landis described a situation in which an adult friend of the family abused a young girl. In a "dazed and shocked" state, she went along with it. Not only did he pass no judgment on her, but he understood. In his own words, "It is not hard to understand. The man was a good family friend, and previous experiences had conditioned the girl to have accepting attitudes. Only a child of exceedingly alert judgment and quick perceptions, leading to action, would have been able to evaluate the approach and repel it immediately."[48] Many modern-day child psychologists would agree. It certainly would be expecting a lot from a child to expect him or her to resist under such circumstances.

The onus of responsibility for these crimes is 100 percent on the perpetrator. Unlike the child, the perpetrator fully understands what is going on, he knows that it is wrong (at least by societal standards, if not his own), and he decides to do it anyway. Although it is rarely articulated in such blunt terms, he decides that his own sexual needs and desires are more important than propriety, rules, regulations, common morality, or a child's well-being.

Further, the fact that children cannot understand or react appropriately to sex is why, from a legal standpoint, children cannot technically consent to having sex with adults. For consent to truly occur, two conditions must prevail: A child must know what he or she is consenting to and have the freedom to say yes or no. So, in a court of law, children cannot consent. The problem is that most people do not live in a courtroom. We live in the real world, and in the real world, from the perspective of child victims, they do consent. They rarely resist, run, scream for help, or report the perpetrator. As adults we cannot fault them for making the choice they do.

Many of us, especially parents, might not want to have to consider that our children might be confused about and susceptible to sexual advances from adults. We might react with denial (impossible!) or outrage (how can you say such a thing!). But for our children's sake, we need to get past both reactions. Perpetrators are well aware of children's vulnerability; they are well aware that children will not get it, that they can offer confused, innocent kids certain things in exchange for sex. As a small but consistent (and very frightening) body of evidence shows, perpetrators specifically seek out and woo children who might be particularly vulnerable to abuse—for example, those who lack parental supervision or seem emotionally or physically neglected.[49]

. . .

AT THE BEGINNING OF MY RESEARCH, I believed that sexual abuse was usually forceful or violent, something clearly done against the will of a terrified child. I also believed that this was why so many victims were psychologically damaged later in life and why many repressed or otherwise forgot about their abuse for long periods. Years later, I have emerged with an entirely different perspective. Obviously there is something very wrong with the traumatic stress conceptualization of sexual abuse that has been so dominant in the field.

Carl Sagan, a man who knew how to make science accessible to just about everyone, said that scientists often make mistakes, but this is to be expected and embraced. Science has a built-in fact-checking mechanism.

No matter how enthusiastic scientists are, no matter how strongly a theory has been embedded in the cultural zeitgeist, we should always be prepared to discard it in the face of strong and substantial contradictory evidence. Science is ultimately about the pursuit of truth, and this is how more robust theories come about.[50] I believed in my scientific ideals and decided to publish my research.

3

The Politics of Sexual Abuse

WHEN I FIRST BEGAN my graduate work at Harvard, a respected psychiatrist at Harvard Medical School gave me some advice. He told me that I should avoid studying sexual abuse. It was just too controversial, too sensitive, and too politicized. He said that advocacy would always outweigh truth and emotions would always override data. At the time I nodded solemnly, wondering what he was getting at. Once I published my research, it made perfect sense.

All hell broke loose. I was bombarded with accusations that I was hurting victims even more than they already had been and that I was a friend of pedophiles.

I was also vilified by many in my own scientific com-munity. Some colleagues and graduate students stopped talking to me. A well-meaning professor told me to pick another research topic because I was going to rule myself out of a job in academia. Some felt my research had a political agenda, one biased against victims. I was invited to give a talk about my research at Cambridge Hospital—home of the tremendously influential sexual abuse treatment program Victims of Violence. No one from the program showed up.

Unfortunately, when people heard "not traumatic when it happens," they translated my words to mean "it doesn't harm victims later on." Even worse, some as-sumed I was blaming victims for their abuse. Such reac-tions made no sense. I never once questioned whether sexual abuse hurt victims. In fact, I spent years listen-ing to heartbreaking stories about how these childhood experiences left a lasting imprint on their lives, rela-tionships, and sense of self. I had never suggested that sexual abuse was not a crime; from my perspective, there was no doubt it was a reprehensible one. And as I discussed in chapter 2, I could not have been clearer that victims are not at fault. In direct contrast to what many believed, the point of my research was not to minimize the harm abuse causes but to question our assumptions about what the cause of this harm really is. But my explanations fell on deaf ears.

Did I not know, a reporter asked me at the time, that for suggesting sexual abuse is often not a horrific experience for victims, that many comply with the perpetrator's requests and rarely resist the abuse when it happens, I would be crucified? The implication seemed to be that I was naïve. Perhaps I was. I had been so focused on why a popular scientific theory was wrong that I overlooked a perhaps more important question: Why did so many well-trained and dedicated professionals appear to think it was right?

How and why did the trauma model emerge as the central interpretive paradigm for understanding the long-term effects of childhood sexual abuse? According to scholars like Ian Hacking, Joseph Davis, and Allan Young, answering this question would require a social constructionist approach. I would have to abandon the idea that scientific knowledge exists a priori, in a pure state, just waiting to be discovered by unbiased professionals committed to truth. Instead, I would have to accept that scientific theories often emerge through a complex and interactive process, one negotiated by professionals whose discovery and interpretation of data are inevitably influenced by the social, cultural, and political frameworks in which they are embedded.[1] As Ian Hacking explains, the basic idea of a social constructionist approach is to challenge the "taken for grantedness" of an existing theory, to "unmask it" and show its "extratheoretical function."[2]

In short, it was time to stop focusing on the fact the trauma theory was wrong. Instead, I needed to focus on the social, cultural, and political forces that gave rise to it and the purposes the theory served for those who promoted and legitimized it.

As I discussed in the introduction, the trauma conceptualization of child sexual abuse emerged in the early 1980s. What professional theories and approaches to child sexual abuse had existed before then? Having come of age during a time when most professionals in the mental health field acknowledged that sexual abuse is a common and harmful form of victimization, I was shocked by what I found in the historical literature leading up to this point. For most of the twentieth century, many mental health professionals believed otherwise.

Sexual abuse, especially as conducted by people victims know, was considered uncommon. In the words of one widely read scholar, Karin Meiselman, sexual abuse "qualified as a relatively rare event, much more rare than most other forms of stigmatized sexual behavior."[3]

Clinicians apparently came across few cases. Charles Wahl reported in 1960 that "it is quite a rare thing to encounter an actual, verifiable clinical example."[4] As recently as 1975, a standard psychiatry textbook estimated the frequency as one case per million.[5] As no large-scale studies on the prevalence of sexual abuse even existed until Kinsey's work in the late 1950s, and this research clearly indicated that sexual abuse was not uncommon, it is difficult to understand where these assumptions came from. Some believe it had a lot to do with Sigmund Freud and his influence on the field of psychiatry.

During the late 1800s Freud found himself confronted with a number of patients who reported that as children they had had sexual interactions with adults, almost always family members. Initially Freud believed his patients. Not only that, in 1896, with the publication of his classic paper "The Aetiology of Hysteria," he proposed that the sexual abuse they experienced had caused the neurosis (loosely defined, psychological distress and problems) that brought them to his office in the first place.[6]

But Freud quickly changed his mind. In an 1897 letter to his confidant Wilhelm Fliess, he explained, "It was hardly credible that perverted acts against children

were so general."[7] For reasons widely (and acrimo-
niously) debated by scholars in the mental health field,
he subsequently concluded that his patients had actually fabricated the abuse experiences they reported.[8]
According to his revised theory, his patients' psychological symptoms and problems did not stem from actual childhood sexual experiences but from "fantasies"
of them: "I was driven to realize in the end that these
reports were untrue and so came to understand that the
hysterical symptoms are derived from phantasies and
not from real occurrences."[9] What motivated his patients
to engage in such fabrication? According to Freud, they
had "failed to resolve the Oedipal situation"—to trans-
fer their sexual desire from their parents onto more
socially acceptable sources.[10]

Many scholars argue that the legacy of Freud's inquiry into the topic of sexual abuse has been a tenacious prejudice held by many professionals in the field
that victims lie about their sexual abuse.[11] For example,
consider John Henry Wigmore's *Treatise on Evidence*,
one of the most widely read and cited legal texts in the
country. He specifically warns that "women and girls
are predisposed to bring false accusations against men
of good character" and that "these accusations might
convince unsuspecting judges and juries." He therefore

recommends that "any female complainant should be examined by a psychiatrist to determine her credibility."[12]

Although some health professionals acknowledged that sexual abuse existed and was perhaps more common than many thought, they were quick to dismiss the cases as harmless to the victims; the majority of sexual abuse offenses were deemed slight and short-lived. Why? For one main reason: because, as I discussed in chapter 2, victims reported that force or violence were rarely involved and that it was rare for any medically significant physical trauma to occur. As John Gagnon, one of the foremost experts, put it in 1965, "The bulk of sexual abuse cases will be minimal in character. . . . The amount of damage—if any, is limited."[13] A text coauthored by C. Henry Kempe, a world-renowned child abuse expert, argued in 1978 that "most sexual molestation appears to do little harm to normal children."[14] The consensus among most professionals was that the majority of these offenses were essentially "nuisance experiences" and rarely involved the use or threat of physical force.[15] As the scholar Philip Jenkins puts it, "The perception of child molestation was as innocuous as the modern image is threatening."[16]

The belief that sexual abuse did not harm victims was so widespread that for most of the twentieth century, the term *sexual abuse* did not even exist. When cases of adults having sex with children emerged in the criminal and court systems, they were often referred to as "sexual offenses" against children.[17]

In the event an abuse victim reported that they had been damaged psychologically, it was posited that this damage probably preexisted the abuse, that the victim "already has a disposition to neurosis or psychosis in later life."[18] In some cases, experts even suspected that any psychological problems victims reported might relate to why they were abused in the first place. Why? Again, for the exact same reasons I discussed in chapter 2: because victims reported that they were often complicit in the abuse in the sense that they did not resist it when it happened or report it in the aftermath. Although, as discussed earlier, there are excellent reasons for why this is the case—specifically, because children are developmentally unable to understand or react appropriately to sexually toned encounters—professionals at the time came to another conclusion entirely. They interpreted victims' compliance as evidence that the abuse was, in some ways, the child's fault. As an example of this flawed thinking, Karl Abraham, the influential follower of Freud who was one of the first to note (correctly) that abused children rarely resist the sexual acts perpetrated against them, concluded, based on his observations, that there must be something wrong with them, that they were preinclined toward their own violation, that they "yielded" to the sexual assault. "The victim herself unconsciously also may tempt the offender. . . . We sometimes find this seductive inclination even in young girls, in their being flirtatious . . . thus exposing themselves more or less unconsciously to sexual attacks."[19] Lauretta Bender, a famous American child psychiatrist and one of the earliest to research adult-child sexual encounters, found that all the victims she interviewed were "unusually attractive" children who made seductive overtures to the psychiatrists. She referred to them as "sex delinquents" and went on to note that "it is not remarkable that frequently we considered the possibility that the child might have been the actual seducer rather than the one being seduced."[20] Echoing the victim-blaming theme, a book on sex education widely read in 1970 stated, "There is the incontrovertible fact, very hard for some of us to accept, that in certain cases it is not the man who inaugurates the trouble. The novel *Lolita* . . . describes what may well happen. A girl of 12 or so is largely endowed with a good deal of sexual desire and also can take pride in her 'conquests.'" The author goes on to suggest that "she is the temptress and not the man."[21] In fact, between 1930 and 1970, the literature was rife with case studies of "seductive children" or "pathologically needy" children.[22] In short, based on their observation that children rarely resist the sexual abuse, professionals concluded that the acts were, in some way, the children's fault. As Benjamin Karpman opined in 1954, "Generally the fact that a particular girl is the victim is not accident: there is something in her background, personality or family situation that predisposes her participation."[23]

Consider that only forty years earlier, an eleven-year-old girl was brought before a juvenile court for having sexual intercourse with a sixty-year-old man who introduced himself to her in a park. The man was acquitted, as the jury refused to send him to prison "for a girl like that." Based on the transcripts of the trial, it is clear that she was considered the offender; she had caused the incident, and any possible harm that she might have suffered was trivial compared to her moral depravity.[24] The professional conclusion for most of the twentieth century was consistent and clear. When victims reported sexual abuse, reactions included disbelief, blame, and minimization. As one scholar, Erna Olafson, summarized, "For most of the 20th century, when child victims were not viewed as liars, they were labeled as sex delinquents. When a man sexually assaulted a child, it was the victim, not the offender, who was blamed and held accountable for this crime."[25]

Professional assumptions about child sexual abuse began to change in the 1960s. Initially members of the child-protection movement led these changes. In 1962, Dr. C. Henry Kempe published "The Battered-Child Syndrome," a report of a nationwide survey dealing with the symptoms of young children who had been repeatedly physically injured by their caregivers, in the prestigious *Journal of the American Medical Association*. In an editorial accompanying the article, he urged doctors to report suspected abuse and suggested that more children might die from battery at the hands of parents or guardians than from diseases like leukemia, cystic fibrosis, or muscular dystrophy.[26] This paper attracted massive national attention concerning the physical abuse of children (and between 1963 and 1968, every state passed a law requiring the reporting of child abuse). It also spurred research on all forms of child abuse, including sexual.[27]

According to the results of two federally funded studies commissioned to study the topic in the late 1960s, sexual abuse was common; a much higher presentation of abuse existed than thought. In fact, Vincent De Francis, the author of one of the studies, extrapolating from the number of cases found, suggested that the results "shattered a commonly held opinion" that sexual abuse was uncommon. He also noted that most offenses were committed not by "stranger perverts" but by adults familiar to the child. Not only was such abuse common, in stunning contrast to what most professionals believed, he theorized that "the hazards and long-term damage" to abused children were "grave and comparable to the damage inflicted in child battering." He called for a coordinated attack on this problem.[28]

Around the same time, a second group, feminists, emerged to champion the issue of child sexual abuse. In *The Dialectic of Sex*, a cofounder of the New York Radical Feminists, Shulamith Firestone, urged feminists to make the issue of child sexual abuse part of their analysis and to "think of children's liberation from male oppression as being linked to women's liberation," to consider it part of the broader subjugation of women in a male-dominated society.[29]

Regarding professional assumptions of infrequency, harmlessness, and victim accountability, feminists were outraged. In a tremendously influential paper titled the

"Freudian Cover-up," Florence Rush, a leading feminist at the time, wrote,

> What can the consequences of such thinking be? It categorically assigns a real experience to fantasy, or harmless reality at best, while the known offender—the one concrete reality—is ignored. . . . The victim is trapped within a web of adult conjecture and is offered not protection, but treatment under some speculative ailment, while the offender—Uncle Willie, the grocery clerk, the dentist or the child's father—is permitted to further indulge his predilection for little girls. The child's experience is as terrifying as the worst horror of a Kafkaesque nightmare: her story is not believed, she is declared ill, and worse, she is left at the mercy and "benevolence" of psychiatrically oriented "child experts."[30]

Indeed, feminists indicted mental health professionals not only for suppressing evidence of the maltreatment of children by men (a "conspiracy of silence" existed) but for male-biased blame shifting.[31] According to feminists, their theories, "surrounded by scientific aura,"[32] allowed for the systematic suppression and concealment of the sexual exploitation of children.

On April 17, 1971, Florence Rush took the podium at the New York Radical Feminists' first conference on rape to address not adult rape but child molestation. During the talk she quoted from past research on sexual abuse and argued that almost all the existing studies on the subject needed to be discarded; they were biased and flawed, conducted by men committed to covering up and continuing their sexual aggression against girls. At the end of her address, she cried out to a wildly supportive audience that a new approach to sexual abuse was necessary, "a new attitude—one that acknowledges the harm that sexual abuse causes and does not blame the victims."[33]

Regarding such an approach, family systems therapists during the 1970s championed what they called an ecological model for understanding child sexual abuse. While they agreed with feminists that child victims were not to blame, they did acknowledge findings indicating that children were often complicit in the abuse. This behavior was understood to be part of a dysfunctional interpersonal dynamics displayed by the entire family (including a colluding wife). The abuse, according to a family systems approach, occurred because it satisfied mutual dysfunctional needs within the family.[34]

Feminists rejected this approach outright. As part of their agenda, they rejected any focus on the victims' behavior, regarding it as diluting the focus on the offenders' behavior. In short, according to feminists, the offender is always 100 percent culpable for his behavior; they attacked any research or theory that suggested otherwise (for example, research emphasizing the fact that children sometimes comply and/or rarely resist their abuse) as negatively biased.[35] One feminist summarized, "It is important not to forget who is the fucker and who is the fuckee."[36]

The feminists involved in this crusade had an interesting challenge to overcome: how to explain the fact that victims themselves said that they rarely resisted the abuse, that they often participated, and that most chose not to report what happened and kept silent about their experiences? The feminist solution was to conceptualize sexual abuse as a violent crime, to treat sexual abuse the same way they treated rape. As Judith Herman explains in her widely acclaimed book *Trauma and Recovery*, "The feminist movement offered a new language for understanding the impact of sexual assault. . . .

Feminists redefined rape as a crime of violence rather than a sexual act."[37] As Herman herself says, this "simplistic formulation" was advanced to counter the view that rape or the sexual abuse of children was in any way the victims' fault. Feminists also defined rape as a method of male political control, enforcing the subordination of women through terror. In short, rape was the feminist movement's initial paradigm from which to establish views about the sexual abuse of children. As Susan Brownmiller stated in *Against Our Will,* "The unholy silence that shrouds the inter-family sexual abuse of children and prevents a realistic appraisal of its true incidence and meaning is rooted in the same patriarchal philosophy of sexual private property that shaped and determined historic male attitudes toward rape."[38] Both rape and sexual abuse were considered a function of the inferior status of women (and female children) in a male-dominated society. Framing sexual abuse as a violent crime rendered all characteristics of the victim and the victim's circumstances, except vulnerability, irrelevant. In no sense are victims implicated in the production of the crimes against them. In no sense are offenders excused from their offences. Blame for both rape and sexual abuse has everything to do with the offender and the patriarchal society that created him.

• • •

Is SEXUAL ABUSE REALLY in the same category of crime as violent rape? According to what victims have said, not really. It is far more complex and multifaceted. But as sociologist Joel Best has noted, such "domain expansion" has important rhetorical benefits, allowing "claims makers" to build new claims on an established foundation, to delay controversy over peripheral issues, and to galvanize professional and societal attention to the topic.[39]

Public and professional attention soon followed. From the mid-1970s on, the topic of sexual abuse was put squarely on the agenda of both the child-protection and the feminist movements. Federal money began to flow in, child abuse and neglect demonstrations became more common, research grants were awarded, and child welfare organizations' efforts (such as establishing child abuse hotlines) increased. Such initiatives drew an increasing number of professionals into the child abuse and protection "industry." A new journal called *Child Abuse and Neglect* was launched in 1976 and became an important outlet for articles on sexual abuse. Media attention followed. In 1977, an explosive article titled "Incest: Sexual Abuse Begins at Home" by Ellen Weber was widely cited and broadly distributed.[40] The article captured and popularized the growing professional conviction that sexual abuse was rampant in American society, that it occurs in families of every social, economical, and ethnic background, and that the topic had been virtually ignored despite the fact that "many professionals" had seen a correlation between sexual abuse and a multitude of adult psychological symptoms and disorders. Between 1978 and 1982 at least a dozen highly publicized books appeared on the subject of sexual abuse—about half of which were first-person accounts by victims.[41] In addition to books, there were many films, major network-television documentaries, and newspaper articles on the subject. Survey results indicate that by 1980, most Americans reported having seen a media discussion of the problem.[42]

The professional and societal attention that sexual abuse garnered was unprecedented. It not only represented a massive quantitative increase from the past but collectively signaled a complete and total break from the theoretical orientation that characterized earlier attention. It was a new perspective oriented toward harm and victim innocence, one that developed not as a rational response to any solid data but because of politics.

In fact, at the urging of feminists, all existing scientific research on the nonharmful nature of sexual abuse or on participant victims was either discarded or ignored, thrown out not on methodological but on moral grounds. It was assumed to be "biased against victims" and even "conducted by male professionals committed to the systematic denial and suppression of sexual abuse." The body of research that subsequently emerged to take its place effectively erased the past. The new emphasis was squarely on violence, force, and psychological harm.[43]

The first wave of research, conducted between the mid-1970s and mid-1980s, involved demonstrating just how damaging sexual abuse was. What occurred was a "cataloguing stage" of all the psychological symptoms and problems victims reported in the aftermath. They were numerous, ranging from mood disorders to relationship and sexual problems, to eating disorders, self-mutilation, and alcohol and drug abuse, to psychosis. These long lists of symptoms were used to justify more professional interest, research funding, and insurance coverage for treatment. In keeping with the new perspective, these studies implied that sexual abuse directly caused these problems, but, as psychologists themselves often noted, this could not yet be proven. According to two influential researchers at the time, Angela Brown and David Finkelhor, although victims reported a wide variety of effects, including depression, anxiety, feelings of isolation and stigmatization, poor self-esteem, a tendency toward revictimization, difficulty in trusting others, substance abuse, and forms of sexual maladjustment, it could not be demonstrated that the abuse was their immediate source.[44]

One of the first axioms that statistics students learn is that correlation does not imply causation. Childhood sexual abuse (A) and psychological problems (B) were found to be related. Feminists, child-protection advocates, and many professionals were assuming that A causes B. However, as professionals in the past had believed, it was possible that B causes A. Alternatively, it was also possible that some other factor (C) that was not being explored (say, for example, childhood neglect or family dysfunction) was causally related to both.

Feminists, child-protection advocates, and other constituencies committed to helping victims wanted, ideally, to find a direct relationship between abuse and psychological problems. That way, it could be conclusively proven that sexual abuse is harmful, and in stark contrast to professionals' past beliefs, the victim was in no way to blame. This could be accomplished if the precise cause of the harm (the "mechanism" driving the damage) could be clearly identified. Just as doctors know that the damage caused by a stab wound is primarily related to something external to the victim—the sharp tip of a knife ripping into skin and muscle tissue—sexual abuse victims' advocates wanted to find an external cause of the psychological pain and damage victims of sexual abuse reported in the aftermath.

By the early 1980s, a possible mechanism had been identified, one that, if correct, could decisively prove both that sexual abuse damages victims and that it is never their fault. It would enable the field to progress beyond a study of mere symptoms to actually conceptualizing the impact of sexual abuse and developing treatments to help victims cope later on in life. That mechanism was called "psychological trauma."

Ten years before, mental health professionals had initiated systematic, large-scale studies of the psychological aftereffects of exposure to combat. This was a result, in large part, of Vietnam veterans' accounts of psychological problems and symptoms experienced upon their return to civilian life. Antiwar psychiatrists and veteran's advocacy groups theorized that this psychological distress was related to trauma—the overwhelming fear, horror, and helplessness veterans experienced when confronted by the life-threatening experiences they faced in battle.[45]

During this period, for reasons beautifully outlined in Allan Young's book *The Harmony of Illusions*, professional interest in the long-term effects of traumatic experiences grew exponentially.[46] An entirely new and well-funded field of research, trauma studies, subsequently emerged and became enormously popular. New scientific societies like the International Society for the Study of Posttraumatic Stress were born, and scientific publications like the *Journal of Traumatic Stress* were released to meet the increasing interest in the long-term impact of exposure to life-threatening experiences.

During this period, professionals in the trauma field discovered that the pattern of psychological symptoms and problems that veterans reported in the aftermath of combat exposure appeared to be the same as those reported by victims of other kinds of horrible experiences—including rape, natural disasters, concentration camp confinement. The traumatogenic theory was subsequently born, and the argument was quickly accepted that exposure to any event that induced high levels of psychological trauma could directly cause psychological damage (even though this damage might not manifest itself until a later time).

A new diagnosis of posttraumatic stress disorder (PTSD) entered the psychiatric diagnostic system

(DSM-III) in 1980. An individual could meet the criteria for the PTSD diagnosis by reporting a certain constellation of psychological symptoms and problems following exposure to a traumatic event, one that was life threatening or provoked the same intense emotions that life-threatening events do.

The professional ratification of PTSD, a traumatic stress model for understanding psychological harm, was a watershed moment for feminists, child-protection workers, and other advocates for sexual abuse victims. If sexual abuse was a traumatic experience when it happened, a solid theoretical framework existed to explain many of the problems victims reported in the aftermath. Finally, after more than half a century of professionals believing otherwise, it could be proven that sexual abuse directly harms victims, that neither the psychological damage that victims report in the aftermath nor the fact that the abuse occurred in the first place has anything to do with the victims.

The problem, of course, was that initially the link between the PTSD diagnosis and sexual abuse was by no means obvious. The theory behind PTSD did not readily adapt to the experience of sexual abuse as described by victims. The classic PTSD theory states that symptoms stem from an overwhelming event that results in helplessness in the face of intolerable danger, anxiety, and/or arousal.[47] It is a theory well suited to trauma such as war shock and rape and to the (rare) occurrences of sexual abuse that take place under violent circumstances. Furthermore, sexual abuse is less an event and more a situation, relationship, or process, one that often continues for a period of time.[48]

For these reasons, this approach met with criticism from some professionals who insisted that the conceptualization of trauma in the PTSD model did not comport with the experiences of sexual abuse victims. In the words of one representative critic, "The circumstances in the prototypal sexual abuse case do not fit the definition of trauma—exposure to a discreet overwhelming event. . . . Most abuse involves the subtle manipulation over time of children by adults they knew and trusted—the trauma model fits in cases of rape by strangers, but for 'normal' abuse it doesn't really apply."[49]

It did not seem to matter much. Beginning with the work of Denise Gelinas in 1983, articles and books began to articulate the harm of sexual abuse as a form of posttraumatic stress—as a direct function of the trauma victims experienced during the abuse.[50] From then on, adult-child sexual encounters were understood as psychologically traumatic for the child in nearly every case.

Framing sexual abuse as a traumatic event and conceptualizing the harm of sexual abuse as a form of posttraumatic stress disorder conferred clear advantages on sexual abuse victims' advocates. Here was a unified model—accompanied by an associated biology that encompassed a very wide range of distresses, disabilities, and life problems as trauma aftereffects—that could be applied to sexual abuse. One very appealing feature of a traumatic stress model was the unequaled etiological significance it placed on "outside" (external to psyche) trauma; the model located the onus of pathology almost entirely outside the victims. Thus, it supported the victims' innocence by shifting the focus from their own emotional reactions to, or interpretations of, the sexual contact to the contact itself.

Another very appealing aspect of the model was that negative outcomes for the child (like drug addiction) were now understood as coping responses to the abuse, as the "habitual vestiges of painfully learned childhood survival skills."[51] Even guilt and shame, feelings adult victims often report, could now be conceptualized as self-protective coping defenses—not "normal" reactions to the abuse but symptoms of an underlying disorder.

In short, by constructing the trauma model, clinicians and researchers were able to reconcile a psychiatric science with a collective story of a blameless and harmed victim. As formulated, the trauma model supported victims' innocence by locating harm in the conditions of the experience itself. As Joseph Davis, a sociologist at the University of Virginia, puts it in *Accounts of Innocence*, a major appeal of the trauma model was that "it supported the unequivocal moral blame of the offender, including his responsibility for the child's passivity and silence, by locating the cause of pathology in his complete domination. It helped to depathologize and destigmatize the adult survivor's symptoms and experiences by explaining them as necessary coping responses."[52] In short, the traumatic stress model did powerful moral and explanatory work; it preserved and encoded victims' innocence.

By the late 1980s the link between sexual abuse and PTSD had been cemented. And since PTSD was a diagnosable psychiatric condition with set criteria, a large branch of the mental health profession became more interested in child sexual abuse. By this time, the topic had become totally absorbed into the field of trauma studies. It has been there ever since.

This trauma conceptualization helped not only to engage professionals but most certainly to galvanize larger public attention to the topic of sexual abuse. In his fascinating book *The Culture of Fear*, Barry Glassner writes, "If an expert hopes to alchemize a homespun theory into conventional wisdom he must be bold. His best chances of doing so are to engage the public's emotions, for emotion is the enemy of rational argument."[53] And, as emotions go, one of them—fear—is more potent than others. As Richard Nixon supposedly once said, "People react to fear, not love. They don't teach that in Sunday school, but it's true." Consider the fear-inducing implications of the trauma model. As many as 20 percent of our nation's children were "being raped in large numbers," "forced against their will into terrifying acts"—acts so horrific that most victims were "psychologically scarred for life."

Cognitive psychologists who study fear can offer excellent explanations of the kinds of things people tend to be particularly afraid of. For example, negative events we cannot control (like being in a plane crash) are much more of a source of fear than those we can control (like having a car accident). Generally speaking, we are also more afraid of negative events we can easily imagine (like our house burning down) than of those that are harder to envisage (like a pipe breaking in our basement and our house flooding). We are also more afraid of ones that are immediate (like a terrorist attack) than of those that involve a gradual process (like our arteries slowly clogging with fat). The truth is, in all cases, we are far more likely to suffer harm from the latter examples, but they're still not as scary. Given a fixed probability of a frightening event's occurring (like a child being sexually abused), most of us are much more likely to get worked up if it is presented as one that we cannot control, that we can easily imagine, and that happens all at once.[54] The trauma model of sexual abuse is thus particularly well designed to trigger our fear—certainly much more so than the truth that sexual abuse is often a gradual process in which a confused child is manipulated by someone he or she trusts into performing sex acts the child does not fully understand. Barry Glassner emphasizes that immense power and money await those who tap into our fears. Perhaps immense power and money weren't the goal in this instance, but once the trauma model was adopted, a sea change occurred in professional and cultural beliefs and attitudes toward sexual abuse. People started to care about the subject; they accepted it as common and harmful to victims. We now understood that it is never the victim's fault. The topic of sexual abuse moved from virtual obscurity into the limelight of public and professional awareness.

Today, there are thousands of articles under the descriptor of child sexual abuse. Combined with numerous books, conference papers, professional seminars, and so on, the response to child sexual abuse has been overwhelming. Sexual abuse prevention programs have been incorporated into most educational curricula. Reporting laws have been passed in every state. A tremendously influential, federally funded National Center on Child Abuse and Neglect exists. There are hundreds of thousands of professionals—in fields ranging from psychiatry to law, from education to social work—who specialize in sexual abuse and conduct research on causes, consequences, and prevention. Roper polls indicate that 92 percent of the country reports that sexual abuse is something we are very concerned about. Millions of federal and private dollars have been, and are being, put into designing sexual abuse treatment and prevention programs. These developments show that the harsh reality of child sexual abuse has at last been recognized and that a broad coalition has been formed to address the problem.

Social movements, according to experts David Snow and Robert Benford, "frame and assign meaning to and interpret relevant events and conditions in ways that are intended to mobilize potential adherents and constituents, to garner bystander support and to demobilize antagonists."[55] By framing sexual abuse as traumatic, child welfare advocates, feminists, and mental health professionals accomplished all of the above. During the 1980s and 1990s, not only did the idea of trauma become attached to a movement (raising attention to the prevalence and harmfulness of sexual abuse), but it may have been the horse that pulled the cart—the idea of trauma proved harm, preserved victim innocence, and helped galvanize professional and social attention to the topic. As Judith Herman states in the opening of *Trauma and Recovery*, "Without the context of a political movement, it has never been possible to advance the study of psychological trauma."[56]

Certainly, professionals and movement advocates have a lot of be proud of. Indeed, the trauma model enabled victim's advocacy groups in the 1970s to accomplish an important goal: to raise societal attention to the existence and harmfulness of sexual abuse. It was instrumental in transforming such abuse from a backwater social issue to the forefront of social, political, medical, and legal attention. Since it brought an end to denial, minimization, and victim blame, it seems logical to assume that, from their perspective, victims agree that all this societal and professional attention has proved beneficial to them. As the authors of *The Courage to Heal* explicitly state, "The climate for survivors of child sexual abuse is much different today than it was in the past."[57] Given the assumption that victims themselves report progress, it is understandable that advocates do not want to see, hear, or collect any data that might rock the boat.

• • •

A FEW YEARS AGO, I gave a talk on my research at an academic conference. The purpose of my lecture was clear: We need to modify the trauma model and our cultural and professional perceptions of what happens during and after a case of sexual abuse. The trauma model is not a good fit for the reality of such violations. The audience sat silent and stony as I explained my perspective. At the end, a therapist specializing in sexual abuse cases asked me a question. She wanted to know why professionals needed to think about sexual abuse in a different way. Even if I was right and sexual abuse was not a traumatic event at the time it occurred, what was wrong with continuing to believe what we all believe about it?

Today, I am not surprised by this reaction. I realize that many people committed to helping victims of sexual abuse do not really care about the truth surrounding the actual event. The trauma theory's inaccuracy does not matter to them. We do not live in a scientific lab; we live in the real world. And in the real world, based on the paucity of inquiry into the topic, most people associate our current thinking about sexual abuse with progress for victims. Given that assumption, who would want to risk even the hint of a return to a time when sexual abuse was ignored, when victims were blamed for any sex crimes against them, and when perpetrators got off the hook and went on to defile more innocent children? I understand why we cling to the trauma model. Any data that runs counter to it might threaten the progress victims' rights advocates fought so hard to achieve.

The reason the truth matters—the reason advocacy is, in fact, best based on truth—is that our lies about sexual abuse are not helping victims. As I discuss in the next two chapters, based on what victims have to say, professionals in the mental health field have not made much progress for them. Unfortunately, the current climate for survivors does not appear to be much different today than it was in the past. Today, victims still feel ignored, they still rarely speak out about the crimes against them, and when they do, they are still disbelieved and blamed.

4

Why the Trauma Myth
Damages Victims

WHAT PROGRESS HAVE PROFESSIONALS in the sexual
abuse field made when it comes to understanding and treating child sexual abuse? Certainly we have
advanced to the point that some of the right things are
being said (sexual abuse is common and harmful; it is
never the child's fault). Funding in the trauma field has
been secured, research conducted, studies and books
published, treatment centers established, and public
awareness raised through sex-education programs and
campaigns in the media. But is any of it translating into
actual progress for victims? According to a report from
the U.S. Department of Justice, sexual victimization
costs victims and their families an estimated $1.5 billion
in medical expenses and $23 billion total annually.[1] Do

they feel that they're being helped, that they're understood and their needs are being served effectively? The paucity of inquiry into the topic leads to the conclusion that many professionals do not think to ask.[2]

The trauma model's main purpose—one of the primary reasons why mental health professionals welcomed it with such enthusiasm in the 1980s (despite there being so little data to support it)—was to provide an explanation for how and why sexual abuse wreaks such psychological and social havoc in victims. Armed with such an explanation, committed mental health professionals hoped to be better able to help victims cope with and recover from these damaging crimes.

The problem is that today, after more than twenty-five years, predictions based on the trauma model have not proved accurate. Characteristics of the sexual abuse experience related to trauma (like how frightening it was, whether penetration or force was involved, and how many times it happened) do not do a good job of forecasting the significance of the victim's psychological harm in the aftermath.[3] There appears to be no direct, linear relationship between the severity of the abuse and the psychosocial difficulties victims experience in adulthood.[4] Worst of all, we have developed no clearly effective treatments for sexual abuse victims:

They continue to suffer from psychological and social problems in the aftermath, and mental health professionals still have not reached a consensus as to exactly why or what precisely to do to help them recover.[5] It is thus not surprising that recently some medical health professionals have begun to ask what "twenty years of passionate rhetoric about trauma" has actually accomplished for victims.[6]

This state of affairs, I would argue, is far from surprising. How can trauma be the cause of harm if most victims say that the abuse was not traumatic when it happened? Indeed, professionals should have paid more attention to what victims had to say from the beginning. A growing number of scholars in the sexual abuse field are coming to agree that understanding how and why sexual abuse damages victims probably has little to do with the actual abuse and a lot to do with what happens in its aftermath. For example, as David Finkelhor concluded in his recent book *Childhood Victimization*, continuing research efforts that seek to track the consequences of early events through developmental, cognitive, and behavioral pathways may prove more fruitful than continuing the restrictive focus on the severity and nature of event-specific trauma.[7] I believe that the victims themselves have always known this.

• • •

JEN WAS A SIXTY-FIVE-YEAR-OLD, divorced, retired administrative assistant. A tall, big-boned redhead with long purple fingernails, she was up front about lots of things. She did not like the coffee I gave her, my office was too cold (and then too hot when I turned the heat on), and she did not like the color of my hair. We were at the part of the interview when I asked her to rate how traumatic the abuse was when it happened. She did not like the questions I asked.

"Nothing personal," she said, "but these are kind of dumb. If you are trying to do what you say you're trying to do, and figure out why the abuse screwed me up so badly, why are you asking so many questions about what it was like when it happened? What you need to be focusing on was what it was like later on."

I asked what she meant. She clicked her tongue impatiently. "What I mean is that what it was like when it happened and what it is like now are two separate things entirely."

At that point in my career, I did not have a lot of experience interviewing sexual abuse victims. I had, however, a lot of experience interviewing victims of other kinds of horrible experiences (motor vehicle accidents, combat, natural disasters, abductions), and I had asked these subjects to rate how traumatic the events were at the time. No one in these studies had ever said this to me before. And, as far as I knew at the time, scholars were not talking about how perceptions of the traumatic nature of an abuse experience change over time—how an event not initially perceived as horrible could become so. They certainly talked about how symptoms of trauma (depression, anxiety) might not manifest themselves until long after the abuse, but they were not talking about how perceptions of the abuse it-self can change.[8]

I knew I had to consider Jen's words seriously. From that point on, I asked my question into two parts: What was the experience like when it happened? And what is the experience like for you today, looking back on it?

By the end of the study, the data were clear. Al-though sexual abuse was not a particularly awful expe-rience for the victims when it happened, looking back on it, from their perspective as adults, it was awful—ratings of shock, horror, disgust, and even fear were all high. Obviously, perceptions of abuse when it occurs and when victims look back on it years later are en-tirely different. In addition, sexual abuse is very differ-ent from other kinds of terrible life experiences. For example, getting into a car accident is traumatic both at the time it happens and later when it is recalled (although, as memory researchers are well aware, we may distort or misremember some aspects of this experience over time). Sexual abuse, however, becomes traumatic later on. Why? What happens in the aftermath of sexual abuse? I had ample opportunity to explore this question with victims.

As I discussed at length in chapter 2, according to victims, they did not experience the abuse as awful when it happened because most simply did not understand clearly the meaning or significance of the sexual behaviors they were engaging in. That being said, at some point later on in life, they do. Over time, the "cloak of innocence lifted," as one victim described it. Victims reconceptualized the formerly "confusing and weird experiences" and understood them for what they were—sexual in nature and clearly wrong. Only at this point—when the sexual abuse is fully apprehended— does it begin to damage victims.

RECONCEPTUALIZATION

When Anne, a twenty-eight-year-old mother of two, was eight years old, her mother started working outside the home. Between 3 P.M. when Anne got home from school and 6 P.M. when her mom came home from work, a neighbor and friend of her mother's named Frank would babysit. Frank sexually abused Anne. Sometimes, when Anne was sitting in his lap, he would "put his fingers inside my panties and feel me up . . . and while this was going on he would thrust himself up against my butt and he would be breathing heavy."

When it was happening, Anne said she did not like what he was doing but was "definately not traumatized." And she was no different from most of the victims who spoke to me. "I knew it was something I shouldn't talk about with my mother, but not really exactly totally sure why." Anne did know that "he was very complimentary of me, about what a princess I was, how beautiful, how lucky my mother was. . . . I didn't get much attention in those days and it was nice to hear these things." After about eight months of intermittent abuse, Frank left town, and Anne said she "just didn't think much about it again." But then something changed.

Anne reconceptualized her abuse—she figured out the meaning of these previously ambiguous experiences: "I remember this like it was yesterday. . . . I was in eighth grade and my friend Jennie was over and she had seen her brother and his girlfriend making out and she was reenacting them rolling around on the ground and moaning and it was then [that] I remembered what happened; it reminded me of what happened. . . . I realized, totally all of a sudden, that what had happened to me was sexual—that I had basically been having sexual experiences with my babysitter when I was a kid." It took Anne six years to cognitively reconceptualize what happened to her and understand that it was wrong.

For Jamie, it took five years. Her abuse occurred between the ages of eight and ten on Wednesday afternoons during her weekly piano lessons. The perpetrator was her piano teacher, Mr. Anderson. Sometimes while she played he would touch her thighs and "crotch" and his own genitals. She did not like what he was doing and was very uncomfortable, but she did not "really get" what was going on. Because he told her repeatedly how beautiful she was, "Whatever it was, I thought maybe it was my fault, like I was encouraging it." After she quit piano ("not because of the abuse but because I got forced to take the cello"), she says, she "just didn't think much about what happened."

About four years later, the police called. "It turned out that he had done the same thing to another girl in town; she was older than me, and she told someone and they pressed charges. . . . And, oh God, what happened next, it was . . . I had to go to the police station and I had to sit in this room with the other girl and my mother and my father and there was . . . this really scary woman who just kept asking me questions. . . . Did he do this? Did he do that? When did he do it? . . . So I guess then I knew it was abuse."

Here is how Sam, who was sexually abused in the school bathroom by a teacher on two occasions when he was about nine, described the point when he understood the meaning of what had happened to him in childhood: "When I was about twelve and started to get erections . . . masturbating . . . I realized then what happened was about him getting off on me." Beth, molested by a friend's father when she was seven, recalled, "They were showing us pictures of stuff in health class. I think I was in ninth grade, and I saw one of the pictures and I realized . . . that had happened to me and it was sex. . . . It was wrong."

• • •

REGARDING THIS PROCESS of reconceptualization, I am not the first person in the sexual abuse field to note that sexual abuse victims may fail to understand the exact nature or meaning of their experiences until later on in life. Back in 1979 David Finkelhor wrote,

Children may not understand the meaning of the sexual acts they are engaged in, but then at a later time in life suddenly realized that this behavior was inappropriate. Either the children learned more about sex, or they found out that such things did not happen in their friend's families. . . . At that point the sexual meaning of all the previous activity becomes clear to them. Thus, it is our impression that even when a young child at first fails to recognize the inappropriate sexual context of some behavior, the meaning of that behavior does become clear at some subsequent point in most cases.[9]

Lucy Berliner and Jon Conte in their 1990 study noted that a majority of the children they interviewed reported not knowing initially that they were being sexually abused. Berliner and Conte quoted victims as saying such things as "I was led to believe it was a teaching process" and "I didn't know there was anything wrong with it, because I didn't know it was abuse until later. I thought he was showing me affection."[10] More recently, two cognitive psychologists, Michelle Epstein and Bette Bottoms, specifically hypothesized that due to the confusing and secretive nature of the abuse, many victims may fail to understand the meaning of the sexual acts committed (and subsequently forget them for periods), but then, at a later point, come to "relabel" the experiences as "traumatic."[11] I believe I am, however, the first to highlight this "relabeling" as characterizing most cases of sexual abuse—to posit that due to the nature of most sexual crimes against children (not painful or forceful) and the age of most victims (under twelve), the majority will fail to understand the exact nature or meaning of these experiences until some point later on in life.

In my study—no differently from other research—the exact amount of time it took for victims to reconceptualize what had happened to them varied. It depended on the individual victims, on how old they were when abused, what educational and life experiences had taught them about sex, and what kinds of cues had triggered their thinking about what had happened and recognizing it as abuse. Victims described the point of realization in different ways: "A light went on." "It was like, aha!" "I said, 'Oh my God.'" For more than a few it was "like a bomb went off. . . . Holy shit! I was abused!" For many, the realization was a "long, drawn-out process" that slowly built up to a new perception of the abuse. One thing did not vary: only at this point—when victims understood the abuse as such, once they had reconceptualized these formerly ambiguous and confusing events—did the experience become psychologically traumatic and begin to exert its negative effects. And, in stark contrast to our collective understandings of abuse, these effects do not appear to be immediate and direct, and they have nothing to do with any "emotional overload" at the time of the abuse (fear for physical safety on the victim's part). Rather, they are indirect, part of a process, and they have to do with the negative ways in which victims come to feel about other people and themselves. First and foremost, they feel betrayed.

BETRAYAL

When they discover that they have been abused, victims most frequently report feelings of betrayal. As Cheryl, a forty-three-year-old high school teacher on maternity leave with triplets, put it, "I realized that I trusted him, what he was doing, and I should not have. He knew he was doing something wrong, and he knew I didn't know. . . . It was all an elaborate game of sexual betrayal." As Neil, an AIDS activist working for a hospital in Boston, said, "I realized that it wasn't just what he did to me physically. At that moment [of discovery],

I lost my father. He was no longer someone who loved and took care of me. I was just being used by him for his personal gratification."

Sexual abuse victims often feel betrayed for good reason: They *were* betrayed.[12] The abuse is intentional on the part of perpetrators. Someone the child knew violated social norms. Although the perpetrator may have an explanation—he was lonely, his wife would not sleep with him, he was drunk, and so forth—in almost all cases he is still very aware that what he is doing is wrong. As Morton Bard and Dawn Sangrey, two researchers specializing in interpersonal crimes, note, "The victims have been deliberately violated by another person. The crime was not an accident. . . . It is the direct result of the conscious malicious intention of another human being."[13]

For the victims who spoke to me, the degree of the betrayal was a function of two main variables. First, it depended on how close the victim felt to the perpetrator, on how much he or she trusted, cared about, or loved him. Here is how Martha, an art director for an ad agency, described the point of reconceptualization:

The day I realized what happened, I had to think about the experience in terms of how

much this man meant to me in my life. . . . What
he did didn't hurt me physically at all; what hurt
me is psychological, that I realized how important he was to me. I thought he was awesome, a
wonderful man. . . . I really admired and looked
up to him. . . . My whole relationship, my memory, my past really shifted, from just 'those
things he did at night' to complete betrayal. It
was heartbreaking really. . . . I couldn't stop
crying. I was stupid enough to think he cared
about me; I thought he was wonderful, a good
person.

The second variable related to the degree of betrayal victims in my study subsequently felt was the degree to which the victim believed he or she had been
emotionally manipulated by the perpetrator or "taken
in" by the situation. In those cases in which the abuse
was traumatic when it happened (it involved force, violence, or pain), victims subsequently felt less betrayal.
Since in these cases the children clearly understood the
wrongness of the situation, any sense of betrayal arose
immediately. And, because the children understood
they were being victimized, the abuse was unlikely to
happen again (or if it did, the child remained well

aware of his or her victimization). Thus, victims did not have to undergo long periods in which they unknowingly fell prey to, as one subject told me, the perpetrator's "elaborate games of sexual betrayal." As Tom, a neurosurgeon, put it, "For two years, while it was happening I felt good about him. I believed him, all his lies and let him do whatever he wanted. It makes me sick to think about how much I trusted him, how much, for how long he took advantage of that." In other words, the degree of betrayal victims felt in the aftermath was an inverse function of how traumatic the abuse was when it happened: the less traumatic it was, the more betrayal victims reported.

As a consequence, many told me, this betrayal forced them to rethink the past—to question some of their fundamental assumptions about being loved and protected. For many victims, a former sense of security is shattered; many report feeling a new sense of interpersonal insecurity and vulnerability.[14] As Maria told me, "The day I understood what happened to me, I completely lost my own sense of security. The childhood I imagined I had—the safety that enveloped me—was shattered. The people who were supposed to be looking out for my well-being [and] taking care of me were not."

These feelings of insecurity and vulnerability are not confined to the perpetrator and the event. They have global and pervasive repercussions; they extend far beyond the actual abuse situation. Many experience a profound breakdown of trust, not just in the perpetrator but in other people. Comments like this are common:

This taught me that I can't trust anyone, that even the most honest and caring people are probably just in it for themselves.

I always think that they're lying, that nobody really loves me—that they're just using me in some way.

This betrayal affects not only victims' feelings of security and trust in others but also their self-worth. They feel that since they must not have been loved, perhaps they were not worth loving. As Charles, a history professor, explained to me, "You learn that who you are and what you might want or need just does not matter." For many, the fact that someone they loved and trusted had abused them led them to think that this person believed they deserved or warranted such treatment. As

Elinor, a freelance photographer for outlets such as *National Geographic,* put it, "What did he see in me? What was it about me and not my sisters? He could have come after any of us; we were all there. . . . I think there was something about me, maybe because I was too needy?"

Considering the degree and extent of the betrayal victims felt, I expected anger at the perpetrator to be a common reaction. Yet only 5 percent spontaneously reported feeling angry at their abuser. Why would the victim of a crime punishable in almost any court system in the world not be angry at the perpetrator? According to victims, it is because they turned the anger inward. Most, to a shocking extent, blamed themselves.

SELF-BLAME

According to philosophers, psychiatrists, and intellectuals from Aristotle to William James, from Shelley Taylor to Brendan Maher, from Sigmund Freud to Donald Spence, when bad things happen to people—like discovering they were sexually abused by an adult they trusted—it is human nature to want to engage in a search for meaning, to understand why the event occurred and what its implications for one's life are.[15] The

nineteenth-century memory researcher Frederick Bartlett may have been the first to name this search: he
called it "effort after meaning."[16]

As psychologists Ronnie Janoff-Bulman and Camille
Wortman explain, a built-in need to "believe in a just
world"—where people get what they deserve and deserve what they get—may motivate this process.[17]
Other researchers agree. As Melvin Lerner and Car-
olyn Simmons assert, "It seems obvious that most
people cannot afford, for the sake of their own sanity, to
believe in a world governed by a schedule of random
reinforcements."[18] If something bad happens to us, we
tend to believe that there must have been a reason. And
if we can find the reason, we will be less vulnerable in
the future, better able to predict and control what happens to us.[19]

As victims struggle to make sense of their experiences, they engage in an attribution process: they scan
through all the possible explanations they can generate
to come up with the one that they believe fits best. Tra-
ditionally defined, attributions are individual causal explanations for why events occur.[20]

If a victim asks, why did someone I trusted abuse
me? there are, of course, endless possible answers. For
example, he was screwed up or drunk, or I was in the

wrong place at the wrong time. The famous attributional theorist, Martin Seligman, would refer to this
category of answers as "external explanations for negative events."[21] It assigns responsibility for the event to
someone or something else. But almost all the victims
I've spoken with, to some degree, endorse an "internal"
explanation. They see the abuse as their fault—caused
by their own characteristics or behavior. Note some of
the comments here:

> What did I do? What signal did I send that
> made him do that to me?

> Well, once I realized I got fu—ed with by the
> prick. . . . Then I was thinking that I had some-
> thing to do with it; maybe it was my fault.

> I just feel used. Dirty. I think part of it was that
> he knew I was gay and he just targeted me . . .
> like maybe I brought it on . . . like it was my
> fault.

I asked victims who was to blame for the abuse—
them, the perpetrator, or both. Almost 80 percent felt
both were at fault. While almost all could acknowledge

that the perpetrator was responsible, they also thought they had done something wrong too.

Particularly heartbreaking about this guilt is its pervasiveness. Victims feel that whatever it was about them that caused the abuse was not confined to the specific situation they were in (for example, "It happened because at that time in my life I did not understand sex"); instead, as attributional theorists would say, it is global and stable (it extends to other situations across time). In other words, victims do not just feel like they did something wrong regarding the abuse; they feel like there is something wrong with them as individuals, that whatever in them caused the abuse is characterological or traitlike. As Samantha, a veterinarian in her forties molested by her stepfather between the ages of seven and nine, explained, "I think it happened because I was damaged. . . . This is why he sought me out; this is why I responded the way I did. I know what he did was wrong, but I cannot escape the feeling that there is something wrong with me." As Suzie, a twenty-eight-year-old columnist for a popular teen magazine, put it, "People can tell me it was not my fault but in my heart of hearts, you know what I think? Bad things happen to bad people."

I am certainly not the first to discover that sexual abuse victims often feel at fault for what happened. Since at least Lauretta Bender and Abram Blau's work in 1937, clinicians and researchers have been reporting that guilt is a common aftereffect of sexual abuse and that self-blame is invariably its legacy.[22] As Denise Gelinas states, "Guilt plays an essential role in their everyday functioning, self-identity, and estimation of what they are legitimately entitled to in relationships. . . . Victims almost invariably express guilt about the occurrence of the experience and usually blame themselves."[23] In the words of Irving Kaufman and his associates, "Guilt is a universal clinical finding."[24] Researchers rarely articulate, however, a consistent explanation for why victims feel so guilty. If, as trauma researchers have stressed for the last twenty-five years, sexual abuse is something done to a victim against his or her will, why would so many victims feel at fault? Some professionals are content to let this remain a mystery.[25] Others proffer such explanations as that perpetrators explicitly told victims that the abuse was their fault,[26] or perhaps victims want to feel like it was their fault because they feel loyal to their abusers,[27] or they prefer feeling guilty over believing they were totally helpless and had no control over their environment.[28] Regarding this latter explanation, David Spiegel, a tremendously influential sexual abuse researcher, notes that most victims "blame themselves inappropriately for situations over which they had no control. Oddly, it is less painful to think you brought a tragedy upon yourself than to face your vulnerability to mistreatment."[29] Judith Herman offers another explanation entirely: The guilt victims report may actually be a symptom of a new psychiatric disorder she calls complex posttraumatic stress disorder (PTSD) (one caused by prolonged exposure to interpersonal trauma).[30]

None of these explanations even comes close to matching the one most victims give. I've found that victims have a pretty clear reason, one that has nothing to do with anything the perpetrator told them, anything they unconsciously want to believe, or any irrational or psychiatrically disordered thinking on their part. Ironically, many of us find their answer too "politically incorrect" to address or discuss.[31] Victims say they feel guilty because the abuse was not done against their will. From their perspective, they feel that they allowed it to happen.

Here is how Sheila, a third-grade teacher, put it: "I have been in therapy for this for a long time and it is still difficult for me to come to terms with what happened and to accept that it is not my fault. . . . The way I understand abuse is that it is something done to you against your will. But the way it happened to me, I guess I allowed it. So in that way I very much feel like it was my fault."

Stephen, an English professor at a liberal arts college, said, "Yeah the guy was a cocksucker—in more ways than one, and I know it was technically his fault . . . but I still feel involved. I was involved. I let it happen. I could have said no; I was thinking at the time maybe I should say no, but I didn't. I let it happen."

Here is how Chris, a twenty-eight-year-old electrician from Dorchester, Massachusetts, reflected on his experience: "What am I going to say to someone? I gave this guy blow jobs twelve times? I think that is going to make me look worse than him."

Of course, as we all know, children do not have enough information to understand or respond appropriately to the sexual situations they are put in.[32] To reiterate an earlier point, for this reason sexual abuse is never, under any circumstances, the child's fault. Legally, you cannot consent if you do not have enough information to make an informed decision. But when it comes to the victims' experience of sexual abuse, what is technically, legally correct is irrelevant. Rather, it is important to see the issue from the victims' perspective at the time the abuse happened. They feel that they consented. As child developmental psychologists can remind us, when it comes to sexual abuse we need to get rid of our adultcentric bias.

Some victims feel so guilty, so complicit, that they are not even sure they were abused. Sarah, a twenty-three-year-old, heavily tattooed bartender in a trendy section of Boston, wondered, "Can it technically be abuse if I let it happen? You know that expression, about how you can't rape the willing?" Albert, a corporate lawyer, said, "I am not sure that technically it can be called abuse if I didn't fight it. Plus, I took what he gave me. I didn't take them [Star Wars action figures] and throw them back in his face." Britney, a twenty-eight-year-old freelance reporter, explained, "For it to be abuse I think it has to be done against the person's will. The way it happened to me was more like something I would say I allowed." Related to this, it was not uncommon during my initial screening interviews for victims to ask me, "Do I count?" or "Do I meet the criteria" as a sexual abuse victim. At the beginning of this research project, I found these questions perplexing. How could these people not be sure? From my perspective as an observer, it was so clear that they were. By the end of the project I understood. They were not sure they "counted" as victims because they thought what happened was (either all or partially) their fault.

I have found that the degree of guilt victims feel in the aftermath of sexual abuse is indeed strongly related to the degree of trauma experienced during the abuse when it happened. Specifically, the less traumatic (forceful, frightening, threatening) the abuse was while it occurred, the more guilt and self-blame the victims report later on. Those victims whose abuse involved force or violence usually report the least guilt.[33] In such cases, the victims know it was not their fault. One of the victims I spoke with summarized this quite well: "I was bleeding. I screamed when it was happening. He ran away. I got rushed to the hospital. It was pretty clear to me that he had done something wrong, that it was definitely not my fault." As another victim put it, "I wish it was violent. That it did leave marks or scars. Then at least I would have known that it was bad, something bad was being done to me. Then I would have stopped it. . . . I would feel less guilt. . . . I might not be feeling so shitty today."

Victims who report no trauma at all during the abuse (for example, those who loved the perpetrator, enjoyed the attention, or occasionally welcomed the contact) feel extremely guilty. Consider the following comments from victims I spoke with:

I responded. . . . My body responded. . . . He could see that; I could not hide it. Yes, I am saying it—a few times it felt good. For that reason I can never tell anyone. How can it be abuse if you got off on it?

I did not get much attention at that age. My father was not there and my mother worked around the clock to support us. I was a lonely child. I was deprived [of] attention. This was attention and I was desperate for someone to be with. I am filled with self-loathing that I allowed it, that I was pathetic enough to think that was love.

I would have to do this and then he would take me to this store around the corner. Buy me stuff . . . comic books, candy, firecrackers, and so on. . . . As a kid it was very exciting. . . . I guess I knew it was wrong, but God I loved that store. In that way I feel like I was a sick kid.

Does recognizing their "sexual illiteracy"—their lack of understanding of what was going on at the time—not help relieve the sense of guilt and complicity victims feel? Unfortunately, it did not help the victims I spoke with feel better about what happened. Although aware that, as children, they were confused, they felt that this confusion itself was abnormal. They thought that they should have known or that they should have acted differently. Indeed, many victims suffer from "perceptions of avoidability"—the belief that they could have avoided what happened—and that other children could have and did. The degree to which victims believe they could have avoided their abuse predicts self-blame more than anything else.[34] Why? Tragically, part of the reason relates directly to the trauma myth of sexual abuse.

As researchers who study attribution processes are well aware, when people search for the meaning of experiences and events, when we mentally scan through the possible reasons for the negative things that have happened to us, the list of explanations is not infinite. According to a process called abductive reasoning, in our search for answers, the set of explanations we can generate is limited to the set we are aware of.[35]

Today, most adult victims' knowledge about sexual abuse, about what it is like when it happens and how children react at the time, is a function of what they hear, read, and see in the media—the culturally available, standard scripts about this crime. Because of the trauma myth, according to these scripts sexual abuse usually involves fear, force, and threat. The experience is portrayed as terrible for the victims. They are frightened when it happens. They try to resist the abuse. Whatever happens clearly happens against their will. Books, films, and websites repeatedly assure victims that they had no control, that they were utterly helpless. Words like "rape," "assault," and "violation" are commonly used to conceptualize the experience.[36]

No professionals explicitly discuss with victims or highlight the real dynamics of sexual abuse—that victims rarely resist it, often care about the perpetrators, and often receive "benefits" for participating, like praise, attention, and gifts. In fact, this kind of information may actually be suppressed. The preface of a best-selling book, *Secret Survivors*, opens, "This is a book about the aftereffects of sexual abuse. It is not about what sexual abuse is, but what sexual abuse does."[37] It appears to be an article of faith among professionals that you should not talk about aspects of sexual abuse that run counter to the trauma model at all. Florence Rush notes that during her psychotherapy training, she was specifically told not to deal directly with the issue of consent in treatment because the victims "feel too guilty and ashamed."[38] A wildly popular book written for professionals by Judith Herman echoes this sentiment: She warns professionals not to talk about the issue of consent as doing so will likely to make the victims "feel revictimized again."[39] Karin Meiselman, in her influential book for professionals, tells therapists that although the patient can explore his or her guilty feelings in therapy, "the therapist will not endorse expressions of guilt."[40] In *The Courage to Heal*, the most widely read book about sexual abuse, the authors go to extremes to assure victims that what happened to them was against their will. On page 121 a victim in therapy blames herself because at age twelve she said no to the perpetrator, and he stopped. "Why couldn't I have done that right away, at four, when he started?" the victim chastises herself. "I did have the power to stop him." But the authors are quick to remind any victim reading the book feelingly similarly, "Abusers don't stop because you say no. . . . You have less control than you think."[41]

Because of the trauma myth, I am aware of no public information campaigns that say, "Kids don't know enough to say no." There are no books telling victims, "You let it happen, and it's okay. This is normal. You were too good to know bad." I know of no newspaper stories in which the victim comes forth after years to press charges and explicitly says, "I would have done it earlier, but I just didn't understand I was abused until now." Today, as a function of the mental health field's relentless emphasis on trauma, force, and violence and the subsequent embargo on any real-world, practical information about the reality of sexual abuse, most victims' experiences slip under the radar—their stories are ignored, dismissed, overlooked, or denied by the very people who purport to be trying to help them.

What is the consequence? For victims, it is significant. They naturally compare what happened to them with the depictions of abuse in cultural scripts. As James, a nurse, told me, "What happened to me was different from other kids. I . . . well . . . it's hard to say out loud, but basically I let it happen." *There is something wrong with me.* Arnie, a self-employed computer programmer, said, "The fact that other kids were traumatized when it happens, pretty much confirmed that there is something seriously wrong with me." As Denise, a bathing-suit model, noted, "I wasn't afraid. Sometimes I liked it. Obviously something's screwed up with me." *I am alone.* I think Karen's comments best summarize this perspective: "I know sexual abuse is common,

but probably not the kind that happened to me." Clau-
dia explained, "My abuse did not involve such force and
violence. I basically let it happen . . . so it wasn't classi-
cal abuse."

The trauma conceptualization results not only in
victims' negative feelings of guilt and isolation not being neutralized but in their being exacerbated; victims
feel worse. The fact that their abuse bears little resemblance to what, apparently, happens to all other victims
reinforces their sense that they did something "wrong"
or, perhaps even worse, that there is something wrong
with them. They are different from most victims. Consider the irony: After professionals have worked tire-
lessly for over thirty years to raise awareness that
sexual abuse is common and never the victim's fault, actual victims still feel alone and guilty.

Given the degree of betrayal, guilt, and isolation
victims feel, it is not surprising that they also commonly report shame.

SHAME

Shame, as most researchers and clinicians in the field
can attest, is a recurrent theme in the context of sexually abused people.[42] It is an awful emotion, one in
which the self is viewed as incompetent and as an object

of ridicule, contempt, and disgust. Individuals feeling shame often view themselves as damaged and unworthy.[43] Guilt, at least, can be productive as it sometimes motivates changes in behavior. But shame is overwhelming. Unfortunately, most victims use the word "shame" to describe how their abuse makes them feel as adults. As one victim summed it up, "I think the heart of the damage is shame. It eats away at me. It has eroded my sense of self-esteem and my confidence, my ability to love and feel loved. The abuse stopped when I was twelve; the shame remained my whole life."

I cannot offer a clear theoretical model as to exactly how and why sexual abuse damages victims. It is beyond the scope of my research. I can say with great confidence, however, that based on what victims have to say, the trauma theory needs to go. It is not a good fit for most cases of sexual abuse. First, and most obviously, sexual abuse, for most victims, is not traumatic experience when it happens. Second, clearly the harm sexual abuse causes is not direct and immediate; before it begins to damage victims, it has to be understood ("reconceptualized") and that often occurs many years after the actual abuse. Third, the cause of the damage appears to have nothing to do with any objective characteristics of the abuse vis-à-vis trauma and everything to do with the aftermath—specifically, with how victims come to feel about themselves and others and how these feelings influence their emotions, cognition, and behavior.[44] As expressed by Jonathan, a middle-aged English professor at a community college, "The abuse, when it happened, was so quiet I didn't even hear it. Now the echoes of what happened keep me awake at night."

A growing body of data indicates that feelings of betrayal, shame, guilt, and self-blame are potent predictors of psychopathological symptoms and disorders like depression, low self-esteem, and PTSD in the aftermath of sexual abuse.[45] They are much better predictors of psychological distress and dysfunction in victims than anything having to do with the trauma of the abuse when it happened. These feelings rarely exist without other similar emotions, such as self-loathing, disgust, self-doubt, sadness, and hopelessness. It does not take a rocket scientist to determine that people plagued by these emotions have a very hard time feeling good about themselves or others on a day-to-day basis. This makes it difficult for them to function well in the world: to build close and supportive relationships, to develop the self-esteem necessary for sustained ambition, or to enjoy activities or interactions with other people. Nor it is surprising that such negative emotions might set off a pattern of conduct that confirms and reinforces these feelings—for example, avoidant and isolative behaviors or acceptance of poor treatment from others (like abusive relationships). And rather than imparting experiential wisdom to victims, each negative experience may serve to reinforce the already entrenched feelings of inferiority they suffer from.

Further support for the perspective that what damages most victims has little to do with any trauma they experience during the abuse and a lot to do with the shame, guilt, and isolation they feel later on in life comes from the fact that in the handful of studies that have specifically tested it, therapeutic techniques involving cognitive retraining—identifying victims' irrational beliefs (for example, that the abuse was their fault) and then helping them to modify these beliefs (for example, by providing convincing information about why it was not their fault)—have shown solid promise in improving the lives of victims in the aftermath of sexual abuse.[46]

• • •

I THINK THE BEST SUPPORT for this perspective comes from the actual victims themselves. I asked them what someone could say to them that might make them feel better about what happened. Invariably they had the same two requests: variants of "I would like to know that this happened to other people" and "I would like to know it was not my fault." Their answers are the tragic legacy of the trauma model that has for so long emphasized aspects of sexual abuse that do not pertain to most victims' experiences.

By systematically avoiding these truths about sexual abuse, professionals have failed to communicate to victims that what happened to them is common and that they are not at fault. Victims still feel alone. They still report guilt, isolation, and shame, feelings so potent and pervasive that they may actually be at the root of the psychological harm the trauma model was supposed to address.

Today, victims need to hear the truth. This requires us all to highlight publicly the true dynamics of sexual abuse—to expose the painful reality that most victims care for and trust the perpetrator (before, and sometimes during and after, they are abused), that they do not really understand the nature of what is being asked of them, that they feel they are receiving love and attention, that it does not hurt and sometimes feels good, and that, for all these reasons, participation is common.

Once exposed to the truth about how victims feel and behave during sexual abuse, victims need to hear, loudly and clearly, why they were not at fault. We cannot accomplish this with platitudes or blanket statements like "You were not to blame" or "It was done against your will." They consented not because they were forced to but because they did not understand enough not to. And victims need to know that this is normal. Although they made an error of judgment—ideally they should have said no; they should have resisted—we must reassure victims that given their age and level of cognitive and physical development, this error of judgment was understandable.[47]

In short, in order to help victims feel less stigmatized in the aftermath of sexual abuse, we must all communicate that they *were* helpless victims—not, as the trauma model portrays them, literally helpless but metaphorically helpless, victims of their own level of development.

This information needs to be highlighted in the form of prevention campaigns, books, websites, and other culturally accessible outlets. Until that happens, victims will continue to feel alone, guilty, and ashamed.

Professionals may fear that raising attention to children's participation in abuse will elicit in others a tendency to condemn victims, but I think we better get past this. Victims are already condemning themselves. Here is the tragic paradox. If the victim's cognitive interpretation of the event guides the process of psychological adaptation after sexual abuse, then the trauma theory is not only wrong but actually backwards. The less traumatic sexual abuse was when it happened, the more betrayal, guilt, isolation, and shame victims will feel and the more psychological distress and dysfunction victims they may experience in the aftermath. And because it is backwards, the trauma model is not just failing to help victims; it is actually causing some of the harm it was supposed explain by simultaneously exacerbating the victim's damaging beliefs ("It was my fault," "I am alone," "There is something wrong with me") and suppressing the information that would neutralize them.

5

How the Trauma Myth
Silences Victims

IT IS OFTEN SAID THAT ADVOCACY is best aided by truth. Rarely articulated is the reason why. I have explained that by mischaracterizing sexual abuse, by portraying it as a traumatic experience for the child when it happens, not only have we overlooked the root cause of psychological harm, but we are inadvertently supplementing it. A further consequence of this mischaracterization? We are silencing victims (and thus actually contributing to the existence of the very crimes we seek to end).

Thirty years ago—prior to the adoption of the trauma conceptualization of sexual abuse—back when many professionals denied the existence of sexual abuse or blamed victims, feminists bemoaned the fact that a "conspiracy of silence" forced most victims to bear the burden of their secret alone. As Florence Rush put it, "Concealment is the victim's only recourse. . . . Sexual abuse is thus the best kept secret in the world."[1]

Since then, the pendulum of professional beliefs has swung widely. Today sexual abuse is widely accepted as common and never the victim's fault. But not much has changed regarding victims' decision to speak out about their abuse. According to a large and consistent body of data, most victims may either delay or refrain from disclosing entirely.[2] Less than 10 percent of actual crimes ever get reported.[3] Consider the results from the National Health and Social Life Survey, the largest and most methodologically sound national study on sexual abuse. Prior to their interviews with researchers, only 22 percent of victims randomly sampled in the general population had disclosed their sexual abuse.[4]

Less than half of the victims I have spoken with over the last decade had talked about their abuse prior to their interviews with me. Initially I found this extremely hard to understand. Why would a victim of crime, never mind a crime that damaged him or her, choose to keep silent about what happened?

I was certainly not the first to ask this question. Why so few victims speak out is the topic of much debate. One widely accepted theory holds that it is because as children they were warned not to—the perpetrator threatened that harm would come to them or the people they cared about if they spoke out.[5] In *The Courage to Heal*, the most widely read book for sexual abuse victims, the authors note, "Abusers say things like 'I'll kill you if you tell.'"[6] The author of *Secret Survivors*, another popular book written for victims, tells readers that victims rarely speak out because they are "terrified by the possible physical harm that can come to themselves and others."[7] Another influential sexual abuse researcher writes that in most cases (of the people she studied), the victims were "threatened with the most dreadful consequences if they told." As an example, she cites a victim named Maggie whose father told her that if she told anyone he would have her shot.[8]

This argument does not fit the data well. In the literature on disclosure, a factor that consistently emerges as *predictive* of whether victims will in fact report their abuse is trauma. In the cases in which the victim is frightened or terrified when the abuse happens, when force, violence, or actual physical rape occurs, the victim is much more likely to speak out.[9] If the source of silence is fear of physical harm, why would the very crimes that actually involve physical harm be the ones victims choose to disclose? It does not make sense.

According to what victims say, this is because the argument is wrong. As children, they do not speak out because they do not know they should; they fail to fully understand the meaning or significance of the activities they are being asked to engage in. As I discussed in chapter 2, many can sense that there is something wrong with these activities, but they are not sure what. As one victim put it to me, "As a kid it was like a double bind. I didn't know enough to justify saying no to someone like him, but I did know enough to know I probably shouldn't tell anyone. . . . I was stuck in the middle."

As adults, victims say they do not disclose for different reasons. Later in life, as I discussed in chapter 4, they do come to understand that what happened was wrong and that they should have spoken out (and most certainly should not have participated). But since they remained silent and did participate, as adults, they feel tremendously ashamed and guilty. Many subjects told me that they feared these feelings might be confirmed if they told others—that they would be blamed. John, a carpenter who had sex with a teacher when he was a boy, said, "What am I supposed to say? The truth? I masturbated the guy after school and then he would give me five dollars? People are going to think I am more f—ed up than him . . . a prostitute." Most also expressed concern that they might not be believed. As Claire, a twenty-four-year-old woman abused at age eight by a well-known pediatrician at a children's hospital, said, "Who is going to believe me? The man is a hero to so many people; he is successful, important. . . . Who am I? A waitress . . . with a GED and a drinking problem." Almost all worry that telling will have negative consequences for their lives:

My family will treat me differently.

It will definitely be very embarrassing and affect how other people view me.

If anyone at work found out . . . what would that do to my partner track at the firm?

Plagued by persistent and pervasive feelings of guilt, isolation, shame, and aberration, most victims choose to hide what happened rather than risk having others confirm or exacerbate the stigma they already feel. Victims are afraid to speak out—afraid not for their physical, but for their psychological, well-being. In the words of Ross Cheit, a Brown University professor who publicly came out about his abuse, "For all this talk about us being a nation at war with child abuse, and for all the media hype . . . the fact remains that it is still extremely difficult to come forward with allegations of sexual abuse."[10]

"These feelings make no sense," a colleague told me recently. "Why would a victim feel like he or she wouldn't be believed or might be blamed if for the last twenty-five years we have as a society been inundated with information about how common sexual abuse is and how it is never the victim's fault?" It is a good question, and I think there is a good answer. As I hope to have made clear, we as a society have been "inundated" with information about sexual abuse, but it is about a specific type of sexual abuse, one that involves trauma. Professionals rarely discuss or highlight explicitly the type of nontraumatic abuse most victims experience—one in which victims are confused and trusting, do not resist, and care for and love the perpetrators. As a consequence, most people in the general population do not know this sort of abuse exists. This is why victims still fear disbelief and blame.

Failure to disclose has terrible consequences for victims. As two influential clinicians emphasize, "There is no agony like bearing an untold story inside you."[11]

The famous psychologist James Pennebaker's research clearly illuminates the importance of emotional expression as well. In short, he says, describing horrible experiences may be essential for psychological well-being. Victims need to be able to talk about what happened—it may be critical to their overcoming the psychological pain they suffer in the aftermath.[12] What's more, disclosure is a prerequisite for access to mental health services and may inform the eventual success or failure of treatment.[13]

Instead of talking, however, victims report engaging in two common coping mechanisms: avoidance (trying not to think about the abuse) and suppression (trying to forget about it).[14] And we need to keep in mind that suppression differs from repression in that it is voluntary and conscious on the victim's part (he or she is actively trying to forget something unpleasant), whereas repression is believed to happen automatically and unconsciously.[15] Whether either avoidance or suppression is actually beneficial is unclear. While some research indicates that avoidance is related to better psychological health in victims, other studies show that people who were able to forget their memories totally for a period were actually less well adjusted than those who always remembered their abuse histories.[16] In most cases, however, neither avoidance nor suppression is possible; the memories are always there. In the words of some victims,

> What happened, it's like a dark shadow, always hanging just above my head.

> The memory eats away at me like a cancer.

> You have to live with it. Like a small nasty pet you have had for years.[17]

The inability to avoid thinking about abuse makes sense. Data indicate that two factors render memories difficult to forget: they are negatively valenced (they make the person remembering feel bad), or environmental cues exist to trigger the memory (reminders of the experience exist).[18] In cases of sexual abuse, both conditions are usually met. Obviously, the memory arouses negative feelings in those who have experienced such abuse. Further, in most cases the perpetrator is someone within the community—a relative, friend, teacher, coach, or priest—and it is difficult for victims to avoid these people, either in person or spirit.

Consider some of the following comments from victims I have spoken with:

> He got invited to every holiday dinner. I would have to sit across the table from him.

> After he abused me he got sent to Vietnam. He died. Every year on the anniversary, there's a mass in his honor. This year my father gave a talk after about what a hero Jack was, how he died for his country. . . . At some point he said he hoped my son would grow up to be such a man. It felt like I was punched in the stomach.

Some victims I have spoken with said they tried to avoid the perpetrator, but doing so elicited negative reactions from other people. For example,

> He showed up at my parents sixtieth anniversary party . . . just walked right on in like he owned the place. . . . It had been fifteen years since I saw him. I left. Everyone was mad. My mother cried. How could I be such an ungrateful daughter?

As a child I coped by avoiding my stepfather as
much as I could. Once when my mother had
too much to drink (she is a drinker, so I guess
you could say that is most of the time), she said
that the reason he left her was because of me,
because I never liked him. . . . She was saying
how could I do that to her, why didn't I think
about her. The worst part of it all was that I
was thinking about her. . . . I was trying to protect her.

The anger, frustration, sadness, and humiliation
victims feel while talking about these experiences is
palpable. In some cases, these emotions build up to the
point that they become, in a sense, toxic.

I was recently consulted by the family of a man
named John. A month before, John had attended a party
with his young son. At some point in the evening,
John's uncle, whom John had not seen since he sexually
abused John some twenty years before, showed up. After avoiding his uncle for most of the evening, John
walked into the kitchen and found him with John's son
in his lap. They were whispering together and laugh-
ing. "It was just exactly what he used to be like with

me." In a fit of blind rage, John pulled out a gun and shot his uncle in the chest.

I definitely do not condone this behavior. John's action was inexcusable. Not only did his rage result in a death, but it most certainly psychologically damaged his son, perhaps for life. That being said, the rage itself was understandable. After all those years of secrecy and silence, of unaddressed shame, guilt, self-loathing, frustration, helplessness, and injustice smoldering away—under such conditions the firestorm of emotion was perhaps inevitable.

The negative consequences of silence extend far beyond victims. Since the vast majority of crimes are never reported, the vast majority of perpetrators go unidentified and unpunished. Instead, according to a consistent body of data, they often commit similar offenses with other children.[19]

As a former elementary school teacher now incarcerated for committing a sexual abuse offense said to me during a recent research interview, "This is a good crime for people who are deviant types. Compared to many other crimes, you have a good chance of getting what you want and getting away with it." When I noted the irony of the statement (after all, he was in jail), he had a quick response: "Oh, I know. I was one of the really unlucky ones. The kid reported it." Based on the data he is correct—he was one of the few who is actually serving time for his offenses.[20]

Given the importance of speaking out—for both victims and society at large—it is not surprising that many mental health professionals and clinicians in the sexual abuse field specifically encourage victims to "reveal their damaging secrets" and "end the cycle of silence." As two tremendously influential clinicians claim, "Telling is transformative. . . . Speaking out is a powerful step toward personal liberation, healing and social change."[21] With regard to the fears and concerns that prevent victims from disclosing, they must come to believe that they "should be as unafraid, unashamed and as unstigmatized by others as a mugging victim."[22]

We idealistically assume that as victims become empowered to speak out, other people will respond appropriately and support them. Unfortunately, in the real world, this is not the case. According to victims, when they do speak out (most often to family members), the following three reactions invariably occur.

DISBELIEF/DENIAL

I told my mother. . . . My heart was pounding.

When I was finished she said that [it] did not happen, that I was making it up. I was shocked. I said "Why would I make such a thing up?" She said, "Maybe your therapist has been implanting some strange ideas in your head." . . . She just kept saying over and over that it did not happen, it did not happen. Finally, I was just like . . . "'Why are you so sure?" She said, "Because I am your mother and I would have known."

Victims are particularly likely to face disbelief in cases in which the perpetrator appears trustworthy, respectable, and successful. In the words of one victim, "They said a person like that would not have done such a thing." Victims also tend to confront denials in cases when there is a delay in disclosure, a long period between when the abuse occurred and when they actually reported it: "My mother kept asking the same thing: 'If it happened, why did you wait so long to tell anyone?'"

Professionals in the sexual abuse field have attempted to surmount this issue by popularizing the theory that victims often wait so long to report their abuse because they have repressed it; as children the abuse was so traumatic when it occurred that their minds erased the memories as a form of psychic protection.[23] As Sandra, a flight attendant, put it, "I didn't remember it until I was in therapy. I told him [the therapist] it was because I think I just didn't think about it until he asked me if I had been abused. . . . But he said the reason I didn't think about it was because it was so traumatic when it happened that my little mind repressed it. Anyway, that's what the lawyer who is handling my case says too."

However, as I've explained, most research shows that the more traumatic an event is, the more likely it is to be remembered. Further, there is no clear neurobiological evidence that repression (the mind immediately and automatically erasing a memory) is even possible.[24] As a consequence, many scholars and researchers doubt whether repression actually exists and have spoken out vociferously against this belief in popular books and media appearances.[25] Hence, trauma professionals' endorsement of repression as an explanation for victims' common delay in disclosure—and as a way to increase the believability of victims' accounts—has done little practical service to actual victims.

BLAME

Even if victims are believed, many then get blamed for the abuse. Again, victims' own words best highlight this terrible result of disclosure:

They said if it happened I must have done something to encourage it. . . . I was, like, what could I have done? I was eight. They said . . . I was always after him for attention, following him around like a puppy.

On the good side people believed me . . . [and were] totally angry with him. But the bad part was that they were also mad at me. They were saying, "Why would you have allowed that? How could you not have told anyone and had it go on for so long?" The implication was pretty clear. . . . They didn't actually come out and say it, but it was clear that they thought I deserved some degree of blame too.

I told my sister first. I thought that maybe it might have happened to her too—her bedroom was right next to mine; we were only a year apart. . . . She said it did not happen to her, and she was clearly disgusted. . . . She asked me, how could I have done such a thing?

My parents asked me, "If it happened, why didn't you tell anyone? Why would you have

waited for so long?" Basically the fact that I
waited so long to tell anyone was taken as evidence that I must have liked it, or something
like that.

Feminists and other sexual abuse victims' advocates in
the 1970s were well aware that our culture has a pervasive tendency to blame children—in literature and in
the real world. In fact, it goes all the way back to the
biblical story of Lot: "Come let us make our father
drink wine, and we will lie with him, that we may pre-
serve the seed of our father. And they made their father
drink wine that night: and the firstborn went in, and
lay with her father; and he perceived not when she lay
down, nor when she arose."[26]

In *Lolita*, Vladimir Nabokov's famous fictional account of a middle aged man's sexual experiences with a
young girl, it is clearly the child who initiates the sexual activity. "I had thought that months, perhaps years,
would elapse before I dared to reveal myself to Dolores
Haze, but by six she was wide awake, and by six fifteen
we were technically lovers. I am going to tell you something strange; it was she who seduced me."

Details of her seduction technique are provided.
"She put her mouth to my ear—but for quite awhile my

mind could not separate into words the hot thunder of her whisper . . . gradually the odd sense of living in a brand new, mad new dream world, where everything was permissible came over me as I realized what she was suggesting."

As depicted by Nabokov, it is the adult who is confused and not the child. When he hesitates, she climbs onto him and says, "Okay, this is where we start."[27]

Here are the words of Lauretta Bender, an eminent researcher in the child sexual abuse field, from 1937: "These children undoubtedly do not deserve completely the cloak of innocence with which they have been endowed by moralists, social reformists and legislation. Frequently we consider the possibility that the child might have been the actual seducer rather than the one innocently seduced."[28]

In fact, this tendency to ascribe blame to victims, to place some or all the moral opprobrium for these crimes onto the child, was a main impetus behind the social movement feminists and child welfare advocates began in the 1970s. Unfortunately, it is still alive and well today. Most studies on blame attribution indicate that culpability continues to be distributed between the child and the offender. According to a series of studies published in the 1990s (conducted using different types of subject populations, involving actual cases of sexual abuse), only 12 percent of subjects exposed to accounts of sexual abuse held the offender entirely responsible.[29] Particularly disheartening about this information is that even individuals in the legal, criminal, and mental health fields were unlikely to attribute total blame to the perpetrator. In the words of one expert, Rebecca Bolen, "The consistency of a victim-blame factor . . . suggests that some professionals still hold the victim partially responsible. . . . It is of further concern that the type of behavior the child displays (i.e., whether the child is considered encouraging, passive or resistant during the abuse) is related to attribution of responsibility."[30]

The following commonly asked questions capture aspects of sexual abuse that other people find particularly potent indicators of the child's culpability:

Why did the child not say no?

Why did it happen multiple times?

Why did the child not tell anyone right after it happened?

Why did the child continue to care about the perpetrator?

MINIMIZATION

In the unusual cases in which victims manage to be believed and not blamed, the significance of the abuse experiences is minimized or overlooked. Victims have reported,

My father said, "What's the big deal? So he played with your hoohoo. . . . What's the harm of such a thing? . . . Just let it go."

Can you believe they actually laughed? . . . My mother said she knew there was something strange about that summer camp. . . . My mother said, "What do you want us to do about it now? Call? Hello, I'd like to report a blow job that occurred in 1979. One of your counselors was a pervert?" They seemed to think that was actually funny.

We met in my therapist's office. She wanted to make sure there was a supportive environment. . . .

They listened. They believed me but they also made it clear that they didn't think it was too important, like what was the point of bringing it up now? Why do we have to be rehashing something that happened so long ago?

I told my parents . . . but then they never mentioned it again. It was like it did not happen. The message to me was clear—to not bring it up. . . . They still invite him to family events; he is still part of the family. So either they don't believe me or they don't care.

According to studies conducted by psychologists who examine jury members' reactions to sexual abuse cases in the court system, this tendency to minimize the importance of sexual abuse is common—especially in cases in which the abuse does not involve force or violence.[31] Abuse cases that involve blood and pain, rape and torture, are far more likely to elicit sympathetic reactions than those that most accurately represent what actually tends to occur. As a litigator who works for a law firm that has represented abuse victims told me during an anonymous interview, "Our duty is to figure out a way to depict the actual abuse case in as horrible sounding a way as possible—to turn what might be perceived as an innocuous event into something that will cause juries to gasp with shock. Did the priest touch the boy's ass? Yes. But don't say that. You need to say 'repeated anal molestation.' . . . Did the girl get her genitals touched a few times by her neighbor? Say, call it 'multiple sexual assaults' . . . that sort of thing. That is what gets attention and sympathy. That is what gets the perpetrator punished."

• • •

SOME VICTIMS EXPERIENCE all three reactions—denial, blame, and minimization—at the same time: "First she said it did not happen; I was making it up. . . . Then after she thought about it for a while she said if it did happen she would have known. . . . Then she came back at me and said what did I do to encourage it, that he was a good man, what did I do? Then she said, 'Well, you seem fine to me. It must not have been that bad. Let's not talk about it again.'"

Such reactions can be devastating for victims. Not only do their damaging feelings of guilt, shame, betrayal, helplessness, and frustration get confirmed, but they intensify. In a very real sense, the person is victimized twice, first by the perpetrator and then by those they turn to for help.

In 1979, Florence Rush wrote that she "discovered that victims were as shocked and disturbed by the lack of sympathy and acknowledgement of the problem as by the incidents of sexual abuse itself."[32] I do not think much has changed. All victims who participated in my research were asked the same question at the end of our work together: What was the worst part of the sexual abuse? Those who had disclosed the abuse to someone else prior to our interview always gave the same answer. The worst part of the sexual abuse was how other people reacted. According to one recent study, the first to investigate the psychological impact of disclosure on victims, the intensity of negative emotions some victims experience during the process of disclosure might actually cause posttraumatic stress disorder in the aftermath.[33]

Researchers do not focus exclusively on damage; some concentrate on resilience (why some victims can emerge from sexual abuse unscathed while others fall apart). It turns out that there is an inverse relationship between psychological damage and social support. The more support victims receive from others (belief, caring, empathy, attention) the less negative the psychological consequences are. Social support from mothers emerges as one of the most potent predictors of outcome.[34]

This is perhaps not surprising. In 1956, Harry Harlow published a classic article, "Love in Infant Monkeys," in *Scientific American*. Harlow separated baby monkeys from their mothers and put them into cages with artificial mothers. The babies were given a choice of fake mothers. One was made of wire with a rubber nipple that provided milk for the baby. The other had no nipple but was made of soft cloth. The monkey infants had a clear preference for the cloth mother, even though this choice resulted in malnutrition. They clung to her, especially when tired and frightened. Harlow argued that monkeys were motivated by a need more for emotional comfort and security than for food.[35]

In subsequent studies, data emerged that indicates that not only was this social support important to the monkey children, but in its absence, when emotional deprivation occurred, the monkeys became damaged—unable to form healthy attachments with others, prone to anxiety and aggression, and unable to care for their own infants when they became mothers themselves.[36]

Studies like these have clear implications for the human requirement for social support. John Bowlby drew attention to the fundamental role of attachment and support in humans after he observed the damage done to children emotionally neglected by their parents.[37] As object relations theorists believe, attachments between children and their caretakers are critical to psychological health. Children (at all ages) need and thrive on intimate, affectionate, and secure relationships with their caretakers. From this, they receive protection, recognition, and acceptance, all of which are necessary to the development of their sense of self-worth, security, and identity.[38]

When such a relationship is not provided, especially during times of emotional crisis for the child, support systems break down. This can have an enormous impact on the child's emotional development, self-esteem, and subsequent relationships with others. In other words, unsupportive reactions, especially from caretakers, as victims believe and research supports, can be psychologically damaging.

What victims need and want from others, in their own words, is very simple—acknowledgment and empathy:

I just want to have it acknowledged, to hear, "Yes, I believe you."

Why can't they just admit it happened? I don't care if he goes to jail; I just want people to know it happened, to finally have it acknowledged and not hidden and covered up.

The most powerful thing a person can say to me is so simple. I am so sorry that happened.

Joanelle was one of the few victims I spoke with who was lucky enough to receive the right kind of response from her mother. She told me, "I just blurted it out. And how good her reaction was. She looked at me with such sadness and caring and said, 'Oh, honey, I'm so sorry.' It was incredible how much those three simple words meant to me." In the words of Joseph, another victim lucky enough to receive a supportive reaction, "After I told him he hugged me. He kept kissing me on the head and saying 'I am so sorry, I am so sorry.' . . . It was clear to me that it was not my fault and that I did the right thing by telling him. . . . He handled it, I think, very well. . . . I think it is one of the reasons today why I emerged undamaged. . . . If anything I think it made me stronger."

• • •

GIVEN THE SIGNIFICANCE of social support for a victim's psychological health, it is important to consider the reasons why so many people do not support victims—why such damaging reactions as denial, blame, and minimization are so likely to occur.

I think a lot of it comes back to the same phenomena: the trauma myth. After thirty years of indoctrination into the idea that sexual abuse is a traumatic experience when it happens, others besides victims have misconceptions about it. Today, most people do not understand sufficiently well the unique nature of child sexual abuse, its underlying dynamics, and the victims' likely responses.[39] Consider again the common reactions we give to victim accounts like those I am exposed to every day:

Well, why didn't the kid tell anyone?

If it happened, how come there were no marks or bruises?

Jesus Christ, she let it happen for two years? She must have been liking something.

Come on, why would any victim wait fifteen years to tell? Maybe they got the idea from watching [a] case in the news—probably figured they could make a buck too.

I'm sorry, but why would such a minor thing cause so many psychological issues? I can't help thinking he must have been screwed up in the first place?

If people understood the truth about sexual abuse, none of these questions would ever be raised. Given the complicated dynamics of the violation—the age of the victim, the fact that the perpetrator is someone he or she trusts and that force or violence is rarely used— it is not surprising that victims go along with it and do not tell for many years. In fact, it makes sense. And given the fact that the psychological damage caused by sexual abuse has little to do with anything traumatic about the abuse when it happened (force, violence, or threat), there is no reason for people to associate the two.

But most do not know this information. Is it any wonder that so many react with confusion, disbelief, and perhaps even a tendency to blame victims? Nothing the victim says bears any resemblance to the "common and damaging crime" that professionals have portrayed and everyone else has understood over the years. The situation is tragically ironic. By highlighting trauma—thereby emphasizing characteristics of a type of abuse that rarely exists—many mental health professionals advocating for victims to be believed and supported, not blamed or doubted, are fostering the conditions that lead to denial, blame, and minimization in the first place.

•   •   •

ONE OF MY MAIN AIMS here is to call attention to the fact that the dominant professional model underlying most of the research, programs, and policies about child sexual abuse, the trauma model, is wrong. I am certainly not the first person in the field to critique this model; other professionals have emerged to attack various aspects of the theory.[40] But there is no evidence that they are being heard.

As we know, one reason for the collective resistance to changing the trauma model is that it helped mobilize interest in the topic of sexual abuse. It has spawned a billion-dollar industry of media-savvy professionals, academics, publishers, and politicians who have transformed sexual abuse from a backwater social issue into a major social, health, and legal concern. But as I've shown, the social attention the model generates has not resulted in significant progress for victims. How is this state of affairs possible? It is as a consequence of the theory not being grounded in the empirical knowledge base. By overlooking, deemphasizing, or failing to acknowledge the truth about sexual abuse, we have silenced victims, suppressed knowledge of the existence of these crimes, let perpetrators off the hook, and ultimately fostered the continuation of the very crimes we are supposedly committed to ending.

* * *

IN 1977 FLORENCE RUSH wrote,

> As a consequence of existing professional theories, surrounded by scientific aura, victims are being effectively silenced. . . . Any attempt on the part of the child to expose the violator also exposes her own alleged innate sexual motives and shames her more than the offender. . . .

The dilemma of the sexual abuse of children has provided a system of foolproof emotional blackmail; if the victim incriminates the abuser, she also incriminates herself. The child is offered no protection, while the offender is permitted to further indulge his predilection for children.[41]

Thirty years later, what has changed? Sexual abuse is still the best kept secret in the world.

Conclusion

THIS BOOK STARTED WITH A simple question: Why is the experience of sexual abuse, as described by victims, so different from how professionals portray and communicate it to the larger population?

At first, as I outlined in chapter 1, I was led to believe that there must have been something unusual about the men and women who came to talk to me, that they were different from most, that I had inadvertently found a group of sexual abuse victims whose experiences did not represent those of the majority. But this turned out not to be the case. There was nothing "wrong" with the subjects I interviewed; their reaction to the abuse both at the time it happened and later on in life was remarkably similar to that of most victims.

There is, however, something wrong with how many professionals understand sexual abuse; the dominant conceptualization of the crime, which underlies most research into sexual abuse, as well as both theorizing and cultural stereotypes about the subject, is not accurate. As I came to see, while some cases of sexual abuse certainly are traumatic when they happen—the child is terrified or in pain; force or violence is involved—the vast majority are not. "Trauma" is simply not a good characterization of the reality of sexual abuse.

Obviously, I found this discovery disconcerting. I had been taught that psychology is a science and that the purpose of science is to base theories on data. Yet the concept of trauma has been so central to our understanding of sexual abuse that it is believed to be the cause of the psychological damage so many victims report in the aftermath. How could this theory be correct if sexual abuse is rarely a traumatic experience for victims? On the other hand, as historians and philosophers of science are well aware, scientists often make mistakes. As renowned Harvard psychologist Richard McNally puts it, "Many of history's greatest scientists embraced ideas that clearly qualify as pseudoscientific, at least by today's standards. Not only did early modern astronomers moonlight as astrologers, but scientific

pioneers such as Boyle, Leibniz and Newton credu-
lously swallowed all kinds of bizarre tales about the
natural world resembling those featured in tabloids
sold today in supermarket checkout lines."[1] This would
not be the first time a field endorsed a theory that later
turned out to be wrong. In fact, mistakes are part of
science; practitioners must accept that mistakes are
made, learn from them, and go on to build better
theories to explain the phenomena they are studying.
As Carl Sagan said, "Science is more than a body of
knowledge; it is a way of thinking. . . . It is defined by
its passion for framing testable hypotheses, in its search
for definitive experiments that confirm or deny ideas, in
the vigor of its substantive debate and its willingness
to abandon ideas that have been found wanting."[2]

I naively assumed that if exposed to data that ran
counter to the trauma conceptualization of sexual
abuse, people would want to revise their views. But as I
came to realize, this is easier said than done. Since the
late 1970s, a handful of scholars have explicitly argued
that trauma is not a good characterization of most sexual abuse, that the theory is not a good fit for the empirical research base. The problem is not that most
professionals in the sexual abuse field do not know the
truth; it is that many do not seem to care about it. As

Margaret Hagan, a clinical psychologist at Boston University puts it, the trauma conceptualization of sexual abuse "has shown itself to be utterly resistant to facts revealed over twenty years of research."[3]

At best, information that counters the trauma theory is minimized or ignored. At worst, it is attacked (along with those who raise attention to it). I learned my lesson well. When I first published research demonstrating that sexual abuse is not invariably a traumatic experience for the victim—that most victims describe feeling confused and, as a consequence, often comply with their perpetrators' requests—I was labeled a friend of pedophiles or even a pedophile myself. This was devastating. My experience was nothing, however, compared to what has happened to other people who have also voiced their concerns about how abuse is understood. Ten years ago, Bruce Rind, a professor at Temple University, and his colleagues published a paper in the prestigious journal *Psychological Bulletin* arguing that sexual abuse does not immediately and directly lead to harm.[4] Professional and societal outrage ensued. The American Psychological Association called for a repudiation of the article, and public figures like Dr. Laura and Rush Limbaugh attacked the authors for conducting "garbage science" and for wanting to "sexualize our children, normalize pedophilia."[5] Eventually an actual congressional condemnation was ordered in which that body voted unanimously to demean the article for alleged moral and methodological flaws.[6] Based on independent evaluation of the research conducted by the American Association for the Advancement of Science (AAAS), there were none. In fact, the AAAS sharply rebuked critics for misrepresenting the article in the media and for failing to understand the methods they attacked.[7]

You cannot challenge the trauma conceptualization of sexual abuse because of a deep-seated dogma that has prevailed in mental health and policy circles since the late 1970s—a rejection of any information that highlights children's involvement in or compliance with these crimes and a relentless preference for information having to do with the frightening, forceful, violent, and threatening nature of sexual abuse.

Our allergy to the truth is a function of three widespread, persistent, and powerful misconceptions that have historically hindered sustained societal attention the topic of sexual abuse. First, if a victim consents to sexual abuse—fails to resist the sexual actions imposed upon him or her—most assume that the abuse is partly the fault of the child. This, as I discussed at length in the book, is preposterous. To admit that children consent is not to exclude recognition of the developmental and cognitive factors that lead to this consent in the first place. Children should not be held responsible for their developmental immaturity. Today, as cognitive psychologists are well aware, a large body of evidence shows that children are not capable of understanding sexually toned encounters in the same way that adults are.[8] Given the circumstances perpetrators put them in, it would be unreasonable to expect them to act otherwise. Many, if not most, children end up allowing the abuse to occur; to point this out in no way removes any of the opprobrium for these crimes from the perpetrator.

Second, it is widely assumed that if sexual abuse is not a traumatic experience when it happens, it will not harm the victims—that "no trauma" at the time of the abuse means "no harm" for the victim later on in life. This, too, is a gross misconception. Sexual abuse may not be a horror show for most victims when it happens, but it certainly can become so later on in life. As I discussed at length in chapter 4, victims eventually understand the nature of what happened to them and reconceptualize their previously ambiguous experiences for what they were—clearly sexual in nature. What hurts most victims is not the experience itself but the meaning of the experience—how victims make sense of what happened and how these understandings make them feel about themselves and others and subsequently impact their emotions and behaviors. In short, an event does not have to be traumatic when it happens to cause harm later on. It is the retrospective interpretation of the event that mediates subsequent impact.

Third, a disturbing tendency exists among many people to equate wrongfulness with harmfulness. Thus, if sexual abuse was not traumatic for the victims when it happened, if it did not immediately and directly cause harm, many people conclude "not wrong." Sexual abuse is very wrong, regardless of how it affects victims. As the brilliant social psychologist Carol Tavris has written, "A criminal act is still a criminal act, even if the victim recovers."[9] If I was mugged and it was not a traumatic experience at the time, would this mean a crime had not occurred? Absolutely not. What is wrong about a mugging is that a person did something he or she should not have. It does not matter how I reacted. It is the nature of the action that makes it wrong, not the consequences. Similarly, it is the act of sexual abuse and not the damage it causes that makes it wrong. It is time to develop a stronger ethical position on the matter, one less dependent on the presumption of harm and more dependent on the premise that the act is inherently vile and unfair to the child. Adults knowingly take advantage of innocent and trusting children, incapable of providing full and informed consent, for purposes of the adults' sexual gratification.[10] To paraphrase the famous psychiatrist Judith Herman, the true horror of sexual abuse is not in the sexual act but in the exploitation of children by the very people they trust to protect them.[11]

Sexual abuse is harmful and wrong, and it is not the victims' fault. Still, we all tend to be cognitively conservative: When we have beliefs that we like, that make sense to us and appear to serve us well, we are highly resistant to changing them even in the face of clearly contradictory evidence.[12] Today, most professionals and other victims' advocates do not care to think deeply or skeptically about how they portray sexual abuse because they believe that the trauma conceptualization of sexual abuse has, in fact, helped victims. Framing sexual abuse was a heuristic that enabled victims' advocates to neatly sidestep or circumvent having to address these misconceptions in a systematic way. It helped quickly mobilize widespread attention about the harmfulness and wrongfulness of the crime.[13] As it is widely assumed that this attention has been commensurate with progress for victims, many professionals today do not care if the trauma conceptualization is wrong. Any challenge to it threatens the advancement that advocates believe they have accomplished.

But as I asked earlier on in the book, what progress have we made for victims? According to the victims whose stories I have highlighted in this book and the statistics in the general population, they are still suffering, they are still silenced by pervasive feelings of guilt and shame, most crimes are not reported, most perpetrators are not charged, and kids continue to get abused at astonishingly high rates. According to the most recent results from a panel of experts convened by the prestigious National Research Council, no clear progress has been made in the field in terms of definition, treatments, identification, or prevention of sexual abuse. And, as a consequence, the health and welfare of abused children and their families are compromised.[14] Given that a stubborn and tenacious trauma myth was used to frame assumptions underlying the policies and programs developed to treat and prevent abuse, this lack of progress is not surprising. How can we understand or learn from what we refuse to acknowledge? Advocacy, as the old adage goes, *is* best based on truth. It is only on the basis of accurate information concerning the dynamics and the characteristics of sexual abuse that professionals can fashion effective prevention and treatment responses.

Not only are our beliefs not helping victims (indeed, they are possibly hurting them even more), but we are wasting huge amounts of money. Think of the billions of dollars in research funding, treatment programs, and prevention initiatives frittered away on a type of sexual abuse that is unlikely to occur.[15] Even more frightening, the more money we waste on trying to understand, treat, and prevent extreme cases of sexual abuse, the fewer the funds available for real needs—prevention and treatment of the cases more likely to occur. This year alone, thousands of children will be abused. Due to the trauma myth, parents will be unprepared to protect them, and victims will be unprepared to protect themselves or to report these crimes. If they disclose, others will be unprepared to believe them or to react in a supportive manner, and perpetrators will continue to evade justice and commit further atrocities. We need to stop wasting money, time, and energy on the largely mythical hazards of violent abuse and direct it instead at protecting children from the real dangers that they are likely to face. To truly help victims, our theories need to be based on the empirical knowledge—and not on assumptions, politics, and lies (however well meaning).

Acknowledging the truth about sexual abuse has obvious implications for treatment. Harm, the psychological damage that so many victims report as adults, is not a function of trauma at the time of abuse. For the vast majority of victims, the negative effects of sexual abuse are not due to any emotional overload at the time the abuse occurred. Professionals committed to understanding the harm sexual abuse causes need to stop focusing on characteristics of the abuse and start investigating what happens to victims in its aftermath—specifically, the cognitive and developmental consequences of the abuse, that is, how victims cognitively appraise their experiences (make sense of them) and how these appraisals are linked to their subsequent behavior, self-esteem, sexual and emotional development, and relationships with others.[16] With this information, we can devise strategies to address and modify such damaging appraisals through individual therapy and large-scale public information campaigns.

Accepting the reality of sexual abuse also has clear implications for how families and society react to children or adults telling us they have been abused. First and foremost, we all need to believe the victims. That the alleged perpetrator is often someone who seems trustworthy and respectable is not an acceptable indicator that the abuse is confabulated. Further, that a long period of time has passed between when crime happened and when it was reported is also not an indicator that it did not happen. Most victims will not report abuse immediately.[17] They cannot. Due to the nature of the crime and their level of development at the time it happened, they will not understand the nature of what occurred until later in life. Further, once they do understand it, they may still fail to report it. In part as a consequence of the trauma myth, many victims suspect that what happened to them might have been their fault.

Choosing to believe victims has significant legal ramifications. Today, most states limit the time in which criminal prosecutions may be brought forward regarding cases of sexual offenses against children. For example, in many states, once the victim turns eighteen, a five-year statute of limitations exists to bring civil suits forth based on sexual abuse claims.[18] While there are many good reasons for restricting the amount of time victims in general have to report crimes (for example, to protect defendants in cases in which time will degrade the quality of evidence required to prosecute them), child sexual abuse should have no finite reporting period. Compared to most other crimes, sexual abuse is unique; it is one in which most victims will not understand a crime has been committed until long afterwards.[19] Why should they not have the right to seek justice?

Highlighting the truth about sexual abuse also has clear implications for the recovered memory debate: the question as to whether people can forget and then, later on in life, remember (or recover) their sexual abuse experiences.[20] The answer is, conditionally, yes. If the abuse experiences remembered were not traumatic when they happened, the victim should probably be believed. In fact, it makes sense that these experiences might be forgotten. Why should a child remember them if, at the time they happened, they were not particularly traumatic?[21] As I discussed at length, there is almost always a period in which the victim reports a lack of awareness that they were abused and then subsequently reconceptualizes the experience. In all cases of disclosure, the first reaction from the recipient of this news should be one of belief and support.

All of this being said, in cases in which a victim suddenly remembers abuse experiences that were objectively or subjectively traumatic when they happened (they involved pain, terror, violence, or force), then it is possible the victim is experiencing a false memory—that the abuse experience may not have happened. As Richard McNally and other cognitive psychologists have written about at length, there is no clear evidence that events that were terrifying when they happened can be totally forgotten, that the human mind is capable of wiping out or banishing horrible experiences from conscious awareness.[22] Generally speaking, the more traumatic an event was when it happened, the more difficult it is for the person who experienced it to forget about it. Aspects or details of traumatic experiences may be forgotten or distorted (what time of day it was, where the abuse occurred) but not the central part (the abuse).

The implications of accepting the truth about sexual abuse for prevention purposes are crystal clear. Most prevention programs today target children; they focus on teaching potential victims to protect themselves and ward off perpetrators. They do not work very well; indeed, we've seen many of these programs in schools today, and kids are still being abused at startling rates.[23] The concepts and strategies they would need to be taught are too developmentally complex. Even if children can be taught to develop an understanding of sexual behavior (for example to differentiate between "good touch" and "bad touch"), we should not assume that this means they can act on this knowledge when faced with a confusing situation with a perpetrator.[24] Responding appropriately is not only associated with social reasoning but also with the complexity of the task. Perpetrators do not announce, "I'm here to touch your private parts"; rather they disguise and conceal the sexual nature of the activity (for example, by presenting it as hygiene) or encourage the child to think of the activity as mutual ("This is what people who love each other do").[25] In short, the unfortunate combination of childhood cognitive and developmental vulnerability and the presence of a perpetrator who will seize opportunities to exploit this vulnerability renders prevention programs targeting children largely ineffective. As one experts sums it up, "Neither evaluation research nor knowledge about cognitive and social development gives any reason to believe that sexual abuse education programs targeting children are effective in preventing abuse."[26] Given that the situations they will confront will likely be too complicated for them to learn to grasp, it is unfair to expect them to.

Consider the following anecdote: My friend read a
book called *Good Touch Bad Touch* designed to teach
children about sexual abuse. Her seven-year-old daughter understood every word, and they talked about what
the book meant. The next week they went to the doctor.
The girl had been having abdominal pains, and her
mother worried it might be a urinary tract infection.
The doctor tried to examine the child's genitals, but
she would not let him. The mother became frustrated:
"Sweetie, he is a doctor. He is someone you trust. He is
allowed to touch you." "But Mommy," the girl explained, "I don't like it. It feels like bad touch. I'm confused." Her confusion makes sense. Her mother was
confused too. How *should* she respond? The adult finds
it confusing to describe the difference between sexual
and nonsexual touching, between people who are safe
and people who are not (and in my opinion this distinc-
tion is not even possible in cases of sexual abuse). Can
you imagine what it is like for children? How vulnerable they must feel? How confusing the situations they
are so often put in become? Given this, it is not surprising that most existing programs for sexual abuse prevention do not work. As one scholar explains, "It is
hard to consider these programs as prevention. . . .
They are palliative at best."[27]

The onus of responsibility for protecting children from sexual abuse should not be on the children; it should be on the adults who take care of them. And to make such protection possible we need rock solid information about sexual abuse—who the likely offenders are (men the children know), what is likely to occur (genital touching, kissing), the fact that children rarely resist (they're confused), the fact that there will be no objective signs or symptoms (force or penetration rarely occurs), and the fact that kids will rarely report the abuse (for all the above reasons). Armed with this information, we need to be 1) watching our children carefully, monitoring where they are and with whom they spend time, and 2) creating an environment in which our children feel comfortable talking to us—one where they are encouraged to share confusing, embarrassing, or frightening experiences and then supported when they do.

Will this be perfect, foolproof protection? No. There are always opportunities for molesters to find ways to tarnish the lives of young children. But we will have significantly reduced the likelihood of abuse happening. The responsibility for protecting children must fall first and foremost on parents and other caretakers.

Related to this, some experts argue compellingly for a public health approach to sexual abuse prevention.

Such an approach emphasizes public education campaigns targeting families and communities, ones focused on providing information and changing attitudes and behaviors. Using social-marketing approaches, "user-friendly," culturally appropriate, clear, and consistent messages could be developed to help people better recognize, respond to, and intervene in cases of sexual abuse. Considerable evidence exists that the provision of such information, in conjunction with strengthening norms and sanctions, can play an important role in discouraging crimes.[28]

At the same time, over the years I have witnessed a troubling and terrible reality: Many of us do not want to face the abuse that occurs right in our own backyards. With great conviction, we talk about how we must confront perpetrators and punish them to the highest degree. We talk about how, if our child were ever abused, we would do everything we could to call out this catastrophic event. Yet when push comes to shove, we deny it. We come up with reasons why we should not confront it—why it would complicate matters to report a brother, a grandfather, or a teacher we have come to trust with our children.[29]

I've heard too many women, when pressed, admit that they would have trouble sending their husband to jail if they found out he was abusing a young child: "I know, I know, it's wrong, but what do you want me to do? It's my husband. I love him." Too many people talk about their own goals and consider the effects of speaking up, should something happen. We think about our own careers ("What would the people in my office think? I'm finally up for a promotion"), about the people in our towns with whom we could no longer associate ("He's been the teacher here for thirty years. Everyone knows him. . . . He's an important part of this community"), about the fact that a sexual abuse arrest or trial would be in all the newspapers ("I couldn't bear to have our dirty laundry spread all over"). We think about having to confront our own worst fears: "Are other people going to think I was a bad mother? That there is something wrong with my child? Our family?" Many of us think that the victim might not be believed and that the allegations might be tough to prove: "Is it really worth all the pain it's going to cause . . . raising attention to it?" We do not want to think about the horror of being betrayed by someone we have trusted, the shame and stigma that would follow if we had to speak out about it, or the painful disruptions to social networks and lives. So, these crimes often remain shrouded in secrecy.

• • •

CLEARLY, THE PENDULUM of beliefs about sexual abuse has swung wildly over the years, but I have realized that these varying beliefs have more in common than we might imagine. All of them have overlooked the reality of sexual abuse; they have focused time and interest on a type of abuse that rarely exists. In addition, they place the locus of harm related to sexual abuse entirely with the victims. Either they were impaired to begin with or were directly and immediately impaired because of emotional overload at the time of abuse, due to the neurobiologically toxic levels of fear and horror they felt. The cause of harm has to do with nothing other than the victim and the abuse—family, professionals and society all fall out as passive spectators to a victimcentric theory that locates, either directly or indirectly, the source of the problem within the individual. What are the practical consequences of such a theory? Not only can we avoid confronting sexual abuse face on, but we do not have to feel badly about it. Whatever is damaging victims has nothing to do with us; blame rests entirely with circumstances beyond our control, circumstances that we are not responsible for.

John Kenneth Galbraith, the brilliant economist, famously wrote, "People associate truth with convenience, with what most closely accorded with self-interest and personal well-being, what promised best to avoid awkward efforts or unwelcome dislocation of life. We find highly acceptable what contributes most to personal self-esteem. What we like to believe is not what is true but what is simple, convenient, comfortable, and comforting."[30] Of course, sexual abuse is none of these things. Would it not be better not to know? By denying the truth and focusing on theories that are false, we can feel good that we are doing something about the crime, but we do not actually have to confront it.

In *The Culture of Fear*, Barry Glassner explores why we become afraid of things we should not fear. We are all afraid of dying, for example. So why do we not worry about what we might really die of—like heart disease? Instead, we often focus our worry—and money, attention, and time—on unlikely threats (like terrorist attacks). Glassner argues compellingly that psychologically this serves a very important purpose for us: It allows us to express our fears and to feel morally upright—as though we are taking a stand, doing something, acting like caring and concerned professionals and citizens—without our actually having to face directly the real thing that bothers us or to take responsibility for doing anything about it.[31]

Thirty years ago, pioneering feminists and child-protection advocates outraged by professionals' denial of the truth about sexual abuse claimed that there was a cover-up underway, that professionals committed to evading responsibility were hiding the reality about the prevalence and harmfulness of sexual abuse.[32] In many ways, I think these early feminists were right, and people in and outside of fields that specialize in sexual abuse work continue to foster such a cover-up. But this cover-up is not a function of gender—it is much deeper than that, and it implicates all of us. As the influential psychiatrist Roland Summit and his colleagues recently explained, the truth of sexual abuse is so overwhelming that it must be denied. "The truth gets suppressed not because it is peripheral to major social interests, but because it is so central that as a society we choose to reject our knowledge of it rather than make the changes in our thinking and our institutions and our daily lives that sustained awareness of child sexual abuse demands."[33] I believe that the development of knowledge and theories about child sexual abuse is immutably tied to our willingness to face the truth, to accept the reality that people we know, love, and trust sexually manipulate innocent children, and to face the consequences—to expose and punish them.

So, why do we fail to confront the truth about sexual abuse? Not because we do not know it is there. Not because we think doing so is serving victims well, but because it serves *us* well. We do not want to know the truth about sexual abuse. Powerful cognitive and psychological incentives exist to blind us from a truth that, if acknowledged, would disrupt the lives of many people. Like the victim, we would have to suffer. Is it possible that deep down we feel it is better if victims feel betrayed, guilty, and ashamed so that we do not have to?

•   •   •

AT SOME POINT DURING my interviews with victims, I asked them why they were there speaking with me. After all, most of them had not talked about their abuse with anyone else before, so why me? Why now? The answer was usually the same: because they hoped that what they had to say might help other victims in the future.

Their courage, selflessness, and generosity were profoundly moving. Their words inspired me to begin this book, and they have inspired me to conclude with some thoughts here as well. Ultimately, in the end, what victims think is most important. They are the people affected by these crimes, and they are entitled to voice the truth and hear the truth from others. They cannot change what happened in the past, but they can change how they feel about it in the present and what they choose to do about it.

Paul McHugh, a psychiatrist, philosopher of science, and outspoken critic of his own field of research, has said that the mental health profession is capable of glorious medical triumphs and hideous medical mistakes. He explained that the antidote for these mistakes is to listen to patients: "A saving grace for any medical theory of practice—the thing that spares it perpetual thralldom to the gusty winds of fashion—is the patients. They are real." He implores professionals in the field to know their patients for who they are and to reject any theory that would minimize or overlook their experiences—to "build a sound relationship with people who consult us—placing them on more equal terms with us and encouraging them to approach us as they would any other medical specialist, by asking questions and expecting answers, based on science, about our assumptions, practices and plans. With effort and good sense professionals can construct a clinical discipline that, while delivering less to fashion, will bring more to patients and their families."[34]

Victims: Do not wait to be asked. Speak out. Empowered by your knowledge about how and why you were not at fault, about how common and wrong these crimes are, and how you have nothing to be ashamed of, demand to be listened to. Do not wait for societal change to happen. Make it happen. There are millions of you. With enough victims informed and empowered, sustained change is possible. The end of sexual abuse may ultimately come not from the hands of professionals or the institutions they serve but from the victims themselves.

ACKNOWLEDGMENTS

I WOULD LIKE TO THANK THE FOLLOWING:

- The sexual abuse victims who allowed me to interview them. Their courage, generosity, and desire to improve the lives of other victims was the impetus for this book.
- My collaborators in the Department of Psychology at Harvard University and at the Harvard Medical School. It has been an honor to work with you.
- The Sackler Scholarship in Psychobiology, the Harvard Elliott Fellowship, and the Center for Women's Leadership and Development at INCAE for their research funding.

- My family. I will not forget their encouragement and understanding.
- My agent, Susan Arellano. Without her guidance, support, extraordinary patience, razor-sharp intellect, and penetrating criticism, this book would never have been completed.

NOTES

INTRODUCTION

1. J. J. Freyd et al., "The Science of Sexual Abuse," *Science* 308 (2005): 501; D. Finkelhor et al., "Sexual Abuse in a National Survey of Adult Men and Women: Prevalence, Characteristics, and Risk Factors," *Child Abuse and Neglect* 14 (1990): 19–28; E. O. Laumann et al., *The Social Organization of Sexuality* (Chicago: University of Chicago Press, 1994); N. D. Vogeltan, S. D. Wilsnack, and T. R. Harris, "Prevalence and Risk Factors for Childhood Sexual Abuse in Women: National Survey Findings," *Child Abuse and Neglect* 23 (1999): 579–92.

2. C. F. Turner et al., "Adolescent Sexual Behavior, Drug Use, and Violence: Increased Reporting with Computer Survey Technology," *Science* 280 (1998): 867–73; D. M. Fergusson, L. J. Horwood, and L. J. Woodward, "The Stability of Child Abuse Reports: A Longitudinal Study of the Reporting Behaviour of Young Adults," *Psychological Medicine* 30 (2000): 529–44; E. O. Laumann and R. T. Michael, "Introduction: Setting the Scene," in *Sex, Love, and Health in America* (Chicago: University of Chicago Press, 2001).

3. Laumann et al., *The Social Organization of Sexuality*.

4. Laumann et al., *The Social Organization of Sexuality*.

5. V. De Francis, *Protecting the Child Victim of Sex Crimes Committed by Adults* (Denver, CO: American Humane Association, 1969); D. E. H. Russell,

The Secret Trauma: Incest in the Lives of Girls and Women, rev. ed. (New York: Basic Books, 1999); D. Finkelhor, *Childhood Victimization* (Oxford: Oxford University Press, 2008).

6. For a discussion of cultural myths about "stranger offenders," see D. Finkelhor, *Child Sexual Abuse* (New York: Free Press, 1984).

7. C. S. Widom and M. A. Ames, "Criminal Consequences of Childhood Sexual Victimization," *Child Abuse & Neglect* 18 (1994): 303–18; F. W. Putnam, "Ten-Year Research Update Review: Child Sexual Abuse," *Journal of the American Academy of Child & Adolescent Psychiatry* 42 (2003): 269–78; D. M. Fergusson, M. T. Lynskey, and L. J. Horwood, "Childhood Sexual Abuse and Psychiatric Disorder in Young Adulthood: II. Psychiatric Outcomes of Childhood Sexual Abuse," *Journal of the American Academy of Child & Adolescent Psychiatry* 35 (1996): 1365–74; E. C. Nelson et al., "Association Between Self-reported Childhood Sexual Abuse and Adverse Psychosocial Outcomes: Results from a Twin Study," *Archives of General Psychiatry* 59 (2002): 139–45; B. E. Molnar, S. L. Buka, and R. C. Kessler, "Child Sexual Abuse and Subsequent Psychopathology: Results from the National Comorbidity Survey," *American Journal of Public Health* 91 (2001): 753–60; B. E. Molnar, L. F. Berkman, and S. L. Buka, "Psychopathology, Childhood Sexual Abuse and Other Childhood Adversities: Relative Links to Subsequent Suicidal Behavior in the US," *Psychological Medicine* 31 (2001): 965–77.

8. Finkelhor, *Childhood Victimization*; E. D. Schwarz and B. D. Perry, "The Post-Traumatic Response in Children and Adolescents," *Psychiatric Clinics of North America* 17 (1994): 311–26. For data that runs counter to the direct nature of the association between child sexual abuse and adult psychopathology, see B. Rind, P. Tromovitch, and R. Bauserman, "A Meta-analytic Examination of Assumed Properties of Child Sexual Abuse Using College Samples," *Psychological Bulletin* 124 (1998): 22–53; H. G. Pope and J. I. Hudson, "Does Childhood Sexual Abuse Cause Adult Psychiatric Disorders? Essentials of Methodology," *Journal of Psychiatry & Law* (fall 1995): 363–81.

9. C. R. Browning and E. O. Laumann, "Sexual Contact Between Children and Adults: A Life-Course Perspective," *American Sociological Review* 62 (1997): 540–60; Finkelhor, *Childhood Victimization*.

10. American Psychiatric Association, *Diagnostic and Statistical Manual of Mental Disorders*, 4th ed. (DSM-IV) (Washington, DC: American Psychological Association, 1991); for a discussion of what constitutes psychological trauma, see R. J. McNally, *Remembering Trauma* (Cambridge, MA: Belknap Press, 2003).

NOTES TO PAGES 7–13

11. For a discussion of how traumatic experiences damage, see J. Herman, *Trauma and Recovery* (New York: Basic Books, 1992); B. van der Kolk et al., "Inescapable Shock, Neurotransmitters, and Addiction to Trauma: Toward a Psychobiology of Post Traumatic Stress," *Biological Psychiatry* 20 (1985): 314–25; J. D. Bremner, *Does Stress Damage the Brain? Understanding Trauma-Related Disorders from a Neurological Perspective* (New York: W. W. Norton & Company, 1992).

12. S. Eth and R. S. Pynoos, *Post-Traumatic Stress Disorder in Children: Progress in Psychiatry* (Washington, DC: American Psychiatric Press, 1985); D. J. Gelinas, "The Persisting Negative Effects of Incest," *Psychiatry: Journal for the Study of Interpersonal Processes* 46 (1983): 312–32; B. A. van der Kolk, "The Body Keeps the Score: Memory and the Evolving Psychobiology of Posttraumatic Stress," *Harvard Review of Psychiatry* 1 (1994): 253–65; J. L. Herman, "Complex PTSD: A Syndrome in Survivors of Prolonged and Repeated Trauma," *Journal of Traumatic Stress* 5 (1992): 377–91.

13. L. C. Terr, "Childhood Traumas: An Outline and Overview," *American Journal of Psychiatry* 148 (1991): 11.

14. For a discussion of "dose-response" assumption, see McNally, *Remembering Trauma.*

15. Herman, *Trauma and Recovery,* 57.

16. Browning and Laumann, "Sexual Contact Between Children and Adults"; Finkelhor, *Child Victimization.*

17. http://www.aacap.org/cs/root/facts_for_families/child_sexual_abuse.

18. Terr, "Childhood Traumas."

19. D. J. Gelinas, "The Persisting Negative Effects of Incest," *Psychiatry* 46 (1983): 315.

20. Herman, *Trauma and Recovery,* 33.

21. Russell, *The Secret Trauma*; K. A. Kendall-Tackett, L. M. Williams, and D. Finkelhor, "Impact of Sexual Abuse on Children: A Review and Synthesis of Recent Empirical Studies," *Psychological Bulletin* 113 (1993): 164–80.

22. For a discussion of the impact of the trauma positioning of sexual abuse in the popular culture, see B. Shephard, *War of Nerves* (Cambridge, MA: Harvard University Press, 2000); J. Kitzinger, *Framing Abuse* (London: Pluto Press, 2004).

23. L. Thorton, preface to *I Never Told Anyone,* eds. E. Bass and L. Thorton (New York: HarperCollins Publishers, 1991), 15.

24. B. Engel, *The Right to Innocence: Healing the Trauma of Childhood Sexual Abuse* (New York: Random House, 1989), 1.

25. E. Bass, introduction to Bass and Thorton, *I Never Told Anyone*, 23.

26. L. Bass and L. Davis, *The Courage to Heal: A Guide for Women Survivors of Child Sexual Abuse* (New York: Harper & Row Publishers, 1988).

27. For a review of the concept of repression, see McNally, *Remembering Trauma*; D. Brown, A. W. Scheflin, and D. C. Hammond, *Memory, Trauma Treatment, and the Law* (New York: W. W. Norton & Company, 1998).

28. J. Breuer and S. Freud, "On the Psychical Mechanism of Hysterical Phenomena: Preliminary Communication" (1893), in *The Standard Edition of the Complete Psychological Works of Sigmund Freud*, ed. and trans. J. Strachey (London: Hogarth Press, 1955), 2:3–17; J. Breuer and S. Freud, "Studies on Hysteria" (1895), in *Standard Edition*, 2:21–319.

29. For a review of how emotion impacts memory functioning, see D. L. Schacter, *Searching for Memory: The Brain, the Mind, and the Past* (New York: Basic Books, 1996).

30. van der Kolk, "The Body Keeps the Score"; Herman, "Complex PTSD"; Terr, "Childhood Traumas," 10–20.

CHAPTER ONE: What Was it Like When It Happened?

1. Social exchange theorists conceptualize social interactions in terms of exchange relations. The central principle guiding exchange theories is that individuals pursue those social relationships and interactions in which, based on perceptions of rewards and costs, they get the best payoffs, or the greatest reward for the least cost. Furthermore, individuals will seek to avoid exchange relations that are high in cost to them. Individuals, from this perspective, constantly calculate rewards and costs, as well as the perceived probability of their occurrences, and so choose the best possible course of action. (Intrinsic to the exchange perspective is the potential for the use or abuse of power.) For a discussion of how a social exchange framework can be applied to child sexual abuse, see E. L. Leonard, "A Social Exchange Explanation for the Child Sexual Abuse Accommodation Syndrome," *Journal of Interpersonal Violence* 11 (1996): 107–17.

CHAPTER TWO: The Truth About Sexual Abuse

1. Some widely cited national sample studies include D. Finkelhor et al., "Sexual Abuse in a National Survey of Adult Men and Women: Prevalence, Characteristics, and Risk Factors," *Child Abuse and Neglect* 14 (1990): 19–28; E. O. Laumann, R. T. Michael, and S. Michaels, *The Social Organization of Sexuality: Sexual Practices in the United States* (Chicago: Uni-

versity of Chicago Press, 1994), 339–47; N. D. Vogeltanz, S. D. Wilsnack, and T. R. Harris, "Prevalence and Risk Factors for Childhood Sexual Abuse in Women: National Survey Findings," *Child Abuse and Neglect* 23 (1999): 579–92.

2. For a discussion of how to interpret the link between child sexual abuse and adult psychopathology, see H. G. Pope and J. I. Hudson, "Does Childhood Sexual Abuse Cause Adult Psychiatric Disorders? Essentials of Methodology," *Journal of Psychiatry and Law* (fall 1995): 363–81.

3. Examples include the PTSD Symptom Scale-Interview (PSS-I) and the Structured Clinical Interview for DSM-IV (SCID). See E. B. Foa and D. F. Tolin, "Comparison of the PTSD Symptom Scale-Interview Version and the Clinician-Administered PTSD Scale," *Journal of Traumatic Stress* 13 (2000): 181–91; M. B. First et al., *Structured Clinical Interview for DSM-IV Axis 1 Disorders* (New York: Biometrics Research Department, New York State Psychiatric Institute, 1996).

4. D. L. Schacter, *Searching for Memory: The Brain, the Mind, and the Past* (New York: Basic Books, 1996).

5. An average of twenty-five years elapsed between when the abuse happened and when the victims were interviewed about it.

6. D. C. Rubin, D. Berntsen, and M. K. Bohni, "A Memory-Based Model of Posttraumatic Stress Disorder: Evaluating Basic Assumptions Underlying the PTSD Diagnosis," *Psychological Review* 115 (2008): 985–1011.

7. A. G. Harvey and R. A. Bryant, "Memory for Acute Stress Disorder Symptoms: A Two-Year Prospective Study," *Journal of Nervous and Mental Disease* 188 (2000): 602–7; E. D. Schwarz, J. M. Kowalski, and R. J. Mc-Nally, "Malignant Memories: Post-traumatic Changes in Memory in Adults After a School Shooting," *Journal of Traumatic Stress* 6 (1993): 545–53.

8. Bessel van der Kolk is the founder and director of the Trauma Center, a program of the Justice Resource Institute located in Brookline, Massachusetts.

9. For a review of the concept of dissociation, see B. A. van der Kolk and R. Fisler, "Dissociation and the Fragmentary Nature of Traumatic Memories: Overview and Exploratory Study," *Journal of Traumatic Stress* 8 (1995): 505–25; J. Freyd, *Betrayal Trauma* (Cambridge, MA: Harvard University Press, 1996).

10. The fourteenth-century English philosopher and Franciscan monk William of Occam (or Ockham) did not originate the principle of parsimony, but he used it so often in his writings that it became associated with him. It's sometimes rendered, "What is done with fewer assumptions is done in vain with more."

11. For reviews of the definition and purpose of the scientific method, see C. Sagan, *The Demon-Haunted World: Science and a Candle in the Dark* (New York: Ballantine, 1996); M. Shermer, *Why People Believe Weird Things: Pseudoscience, Superstition, and Other Confusions of Our Time* (New York: Freeman, 1997).

12. P. Okami, "Self-reports of 'Positive' Childhood and Adolescent Sexual Contacts with Older Persons: An Exploratory Study," *Archives of Sexual Behavior* 20 (1991): 437–57, quote on 438.

13. L. M. Terman, *Psychological Factors in Marital Happiness* (New York: McGraw-Hill, 1938); L. M. Terman, "Correlates of Orgasm Adequacy in a Group of 556 Wives," *Journal of Psychology: Interdisciplinary and Applied* 32 (1951): 115–72.

14. A. C. Kinsey, W. B. Pomeroy, and C. E. Martin, *Sexual Behavior in the Human Female* (Philadelphia: W. B. Saunders, 1953).

15. J. T. Landis, "Experiences of 500 Children with Adult Sexual Deviation," *Psychiatric Quarterly* 30 (1956): 91–109.

16. Okami, "Self-reports," 437–57.

17. L. G. Schultz and P. Jones, "Sexual Abuse of Children: Issues for Social Service and Health Professionals," *Child Welfare Journal* 62 (1983): 99–108.

18. Vogeltanz, Wilsnack, and Harris, "Prevalence and Risk Factors for Childhood Sexual Abuse in Women."

19. Data discussed in E. Geraerts, "Remembrance of Things Past: The Cognitive Psychology of Remembering and Forgetting Trauma," Doctorate thesis, Maastricht University, 2006.

20. C. Landis et al., *Sex in Development* (New York: Paul B. Hoeber, 1940).

21. J. H. Gagnon, "Female Child Victims of Sex Offenses," *Social Problems* 13 (1965): 176–92.

22. D. Finkelhor, *Sexually Victimized Children* (New York: Free Press, 1979).

23. D. E. H. Russell, *The Secret Trauma: Incest in the Lives of Girls and Women* (New York: Basic Books, 1986).

24. C. Nash and D. West, "Sexual Molestation of Young Girls: A Retrospective Survey," in *Sexual Victimization*, ed. D. J. West (Brookfield, VT: Gower Publishing, 1995), 1–92.

25. E. B. Carlson et al., "A Conceptual Framework for the Long-term Psychological Effects of Traumatic Childhood Abuse," *Child Maltreatment* 2 (1997): 272–95.

26. D. Finkelhor, "Early and Long-term Effects of Child Sexual Abuse: An Update," *Professional Psychology: Research and Practice* 21 (1990): 325–30, quote on 328.

27. M. A. Hagan, "Faith in the Model and Resistance to Research: Commentary on 'Post Hoc Reasoning in Possible Cases of Child Sexual Abuse,'" *Clinical Psychology: Science and Practice* 10, no. 3 (2003): 344–48, quote on 345.

28. Russell, *The Secret Trauma*; see also S. Blume, "The Walking Wounded: Post-Incest Syndrome," *SIECUS Report* 15, no. 1 (1986): 5–7.

29. K. A. Kendall-Tackett, L. M. Williams, and D. Finkelhor, "Impact of Sexual Abuse on Children: A Review and Synthesis of Recent Empirical Studies," *Psychological Bulletin* 113 (1993): 164–80, quote on 164.

30. S. A. Burkhardt and A. F. Rotatori, *Treatment and Prevention of Child Sexual Abuse: A Child-Generated Model* (Washington, DC: Taylor & Francis, 1995), 2.

31. F. D. Fincham et al., "The Professional Response to Child Sexual Abuse: Whose Interests Are Served?" in *Child Sexual Abuse and False Memory Syndrome*, ed. R. A. Baker (Amherst, NY: Prometheus Books, 1998), 279–308, quote on 298.

32. K. R. Popper, *Conjectures and Refutations: The Growth of Scientific Knowledge* (New York: Harper & Row, 1963), 46–47.

33. S. Pinker, "Sex Ed: The Science of Difference," *The New Republic* 232 (February 14, 2005): 15–17; S. Pinker, introduction to *What Is Your Dangerous Idea?* ed. J. Brockman (New York: HarperCollins, 2007), xxiii–xxxiii.

34. J. Piaget, *The Origin of Intelligence in Children* (New York: International Universities Press, 1952); J. Piaget, *The Construction of Reality in the Child* (New York: Basic Books, 1954).

35. Finkelhor, *Sexually Victimized Children*; G. B. Melton, "The Improbability of Prevention of Sexual Abuse," in *Prevention of Child Maltreatment: Developmental and Ecological Perspectives*, eds. D. J. Willis, E. W. Holden, and M. Rosenberg (New York: Wiley, 1992); S. K. Wurtele and C. L. Miller, "Children's Conceptions of Sexual Abuse," *Journal of Clinical Child Psychology* 16 (1987): 184–91; S. K. Wurtele and C. L. Miller-Perrin, *Preventing Child Sexual Abuse: Sharing the Responsibility* (Lincoln: University of Nebraska Press, 1992).

36. Finkelhor, *Sexually Victimized Children*, 31.

37. L. Berliner and J. Conte, "The Process of Victimization: The Victims' Perspective," *Child Abuse and Neglect* 14 (1990): 29–40.

38. J. Ortiz y Pino and J. Goodwin, "What Families Say: The Dialogue of Incest," in *Sexual Abuse: Incest Victims and Their Families* (Boston: John Wright, 1982), 57–75.

39. R. Cheit, quoted in Freyd, *Betrayal Trauma*, 11.

40. L. Cosmides, "The Logic of Social Exchange: Has Natural Selection Shaped How Humans Reason? Studies with the Wason Selection Task," *Cognition* 31 (1989): 187–276; L. Cosmides and J. Tooby, "Cognitive Adaptations for Social Exchange," in *The Adapted Mind: Evolutionary Psychology and the Generation of Culture*, eds. J. H. Barkow, L. Cosmides, and J. Tooby (New York: Oxford University Press, 1992), 163–228.

41. K. Abraham, "The Experiencing of Sexual Traumas As a Form of Sexual Activity," in *Selected Papers of Karl Abraham, MD* (London: Hogarth Press, 1927), 47–63.

42. For further support, see R. C. Summit, "The Child Sexual Abuse Accommodation Syndrome," *Child Abuse and Neglect* 7 (1983): 177–93.

43. J. L. Herman and L. Hirschman, "Father-Daughter Incest," *Signs* 2 (1977): 735–56.

44. For a clear and concise discussion of how developmental variables contribute to children's vulnerability to sexual abuse, see Burkhardt and Rotatori, *Treatment and Prevention of Childhood Sexual Abuse*, 1–16.

45. Berliner and Conte, "The Process of Victimization," 38.

46. Berliner and Conte, "The Process of Victimization," 37.

47. M. Angelou, *I Know Why the Caged Bird Sings* (New York: Bantam Books, 1971), 62–63.

48. Landis, "Experiences of 500 Children with Adult Sexual Deviation."

49. For a discussion of risk factors for child victimization, see D. Finkelhor, *Childhood Victimization: Violence, Crime, and Abuse in the Lives of Young People* (Oxford: Oxford University Press, 2008).

50. Sagan, *The Demon-Haunted World*.

CHAPTER THREE: The Politics of Sexual Abuse

1. I. Hacking, *The Social Construction of What?* (Cambridge, MA: Harvard University Press, 1999); A. Young, *The Harmony of Illusions: Inventing Post-Traumatic Stress Disorder* (Princeton, NJ: Princeton University Press, 1995); J. E. Davis, *Accounts of Innocence: Sexual Abuse, Trauma, and the Self* (Chicago: University of Chicago Press, 2005).

2. I. Hacking, "Taking Bad Arguments Seriously," *London Review of Books* (August 21, 1997): 14–16, quote on 14.

3. K. C. Meiselman, *Incest: A Psychological Study of Causes and Effects with Treatment Recommendations* (San Francisco: Jossey-Bass, 1978).

4. C. W. Wahl, "The Psychodynamics of Consummated Maternal In-

cest," *Archives of General Psychiatry* 3 (1960): 188–93, quote on 189.

5. J. D. Henderson, "Incest," in *Comprehensive Textbook of Psychiatry*, eds. A. M. Freedman, H. I. Kaplan, and B. Sadock, 2nd ed. (Baltimore: Williams and Wilkins, 1975), 1530–39, quote on 1532.

6. S. Freud, "The Aetiology of Hysteria" (1896), in *The Standard Edition of the Complete Psychological Works of Sigmund Freud*, ed. and trans. J. Strachey (London: Hogarth Press, 1962), 3:191–221.

7. S. Freud, *The Origins of Psychoanalysis: Letters to Wilhelm Fliess, Drafts and Notes: 1887–1902*, eds. M. Bonaparte, A. Freud, and E. Kris, trans. E. Mosbacher and J. Strachey (New York: Basic Books, 1954), 179–80.

8. For a succinct review of proposed explanations for why Freud rejected his initial theory (ranging from his fear of scandalized colleagues to his failure to bring a single hysteria case to a successful resolution), see R. J. McNally, *Remembering Trauma* (Cambridge, MA: Belknap Press, 2003), 159–85.

9. S. Freud, *The Complete Introductory Lectures of Psycho-Analysis* (1933; rpt. New York: W. W. Norton & Company, 1966), 584.

10. S. Freud, "Three Essays on the Theory of Sexuality" (1905), in *The Standard Edition of the Complete Psychological Works of Sigmund Freud*, ed. and trans. J. Strachey (New York: W. W. Norton & Company), 7:135–243.

11. For example, F. Rush, "The Freudian Cover-up," *Chrysalis* 1 (1977): 31–45; E. Olafson, D. L. Corwin, and R. C. Summit, "Modern History of Child Sexual Abuse Awareness: Cycles of Discovery and Suppression," *Child Abuse and Neglect* (1993): 7–24; J. L. Herman, *Father-Daughter Incest* (Cambridge, MA: Harvard University Press, 1981).

12. J. H. Wigmore, cited in E. Olafson, "Child Sexual Abuse," in *Sexualized Violence Against Women and Children*, ed. B. J. Cling (New York: Guilford Press, 2004).

13. J. H. Gagnon, "Female Child Victims of Sex Offenses," *Social Problems* 13 (1965): 176–92, quote on 181.

14. R. S. Kempe and C. H. Kempe, *Child Abuse* (London: Fontana/Open University, 1978), 55.

15. Gagnon, "Female Child Victims of Sex Offenses," 191; for further discussion of the damaging effect of sexual-abuse experiences, see Davis, *Accounts of Innocence*.

16. P. Jenkins, "Watching the Research Pendulum," in *Sexual Development in Childhood*, ed. J. Bancroft (Indiana: Indiana University Press, 2003), 3–19, quote on 4.

17. Davis, *Accounts of Innocence.*

18. K. Abraham, "The Experiencing of Sexual Trauma As a Form of Sexual Activity" (1927), in *Selected Papers on Psychoanalysis,* trans. D. Bryan and A. Strachey (New York: Basic Books, 1954), 62.

19. Abraham, "The Experiencing of Sexual Trauma," 53.

20. L. Bender and A. Blau, "The Reaction of Children to Sexual Relations with Adults," *American Journal of Orthopsychiatry* 7 (1937): 500–18, quote on 514.

21. J. James, *The Facts of Sex* (Princeton, NJ: Vertex Books, 1970), 118.

22. L. Ramer, *Your Sexual Bill of Rights* (New York: Exposition Press, 1973).

23. B. Karpman, *The Sexual Offender and His Offenses* (New York: Julian, 1954), 72–73.

24. P. Jenkins, *Moral Panic* (New Haven, CT: Yale University Press, 1998), 32.

25. E. Olafson, "Child Sexual Abuse," in *Sexualized Violence Against Women and Children,* ed. B. Cling (New York: The Guilford Press, 2004), 55.

26. C. H. Kempe, "The Battered-Child Syndrome," *Journal of the American Medical Association* 181 (1962): 17–24.

27. For a review of the impact of Kempe's paper on the child-protection field, see Davis, *Accounts of Innocence.*

28. V. De Francis, "Protecting the Child Victim of Sex Crimes Committed by Adults," *Federal Probation* (September 1971): 15–20.

29. S. Firestone, *The Dialectic of Sex: The Case for Feminist Revolution* (New York: Morrow, 1970).

30. Rush, "The Freudian Cover-up," 40.

31. See, for example, L. Armstrong, *Kiss Daddy Goodnight: A Speak-out on Incest* (New York: Hawthorn Books, 1979); S. Brownmiller, *Against Our Will: Men, Women, and Rape* (New York: Simon & Schuster, 1975).

32. Rush, "The Freudian Cover-up," 44.

33. F. Rush, "The Sexual Abuse of Children: A Feminist Point of View," in *Rape: The First Sourcebook for Women,* eds. N. Connell and C. Wilson (New York: New American Library, 1974), 64–75.

34. H. Giarretto, "The Treatment of Father-Daughter Incest: A Psycho-Social Approach," *Children Today* (July–August 1976): 2; K. Sturkie, "Treating Incest Victims and Their Families," in *Incest As Child Abuse,* eds. B. J. Vander Mey and R. L. Neff (New York: Praeger, 1986), 126–65.

35. See Olafson, Corwin, and Summit, "Modern History of Child Sexual Abuse Awareness."

36. See, for example, A. C. Salter, *Pedophiles, Rapists, and Other Sex Offenders: Who They Are, How They Operate, and How We Can Protect Ourselves and Our Children* (New York: Basic Books, 2003), 57.

37. J. Herman, *Trauma and Recovery: The Aftermath of Violence—from Domestic Abuse to Political Terror* (New York: Basic Books, 1997), 30.

38. Brownmiller, *Against Our Will*, 281.

39. J. Best, *Threatened Children: Rhetoric and Concern About Child Victims* (Chicago: University of Chicago Press, 1990).

40. E. Weber, "Incest: Sexual Abuse Begins At Home," *Ms.* 5 (April 1977): 64.

41. Some of the groundbreaking work on sexual abuse that emerged in the late 1970s and early 1980s includes C. V. Allen, *Daddy's Girl* (New York: Wyndham, 1980); Armstrong, *Kiss Daddy Goodnight*; S. Butler, *Conspiracy of Silence* (San Francisco: New Glide, 1978); B. Justice and R. Justice, *The Broken Taboo* (New York: Human Sciences, 1979); Meiselman, *Incest*; F. Rush, *The Best Kept Secret* (New York: Prentice Hall, 1980).

42. Cited in D. Finkelhor, *Child Sexual Abuse* (New York: Free Press, 1984).

43. Breaks in thought are never clean. Some of the influential studies of the mid- to late 1970s might be thought of as transitional with respect to the older literature (e.g., Justice and Justice, *The Broken Taboo*, and Meiselman, *Incest*).

44. A. Brown and D. Finkelhor, "The Impact of Child Sexual Abuse: A Review of the Research," *Psychological Bulletin* 99 (1986): 66–77.

45. For a review, see Herman, *Trauma and Recovery*.

46. A. Young, *The Harmony of Illusions: Inventing Post-Traumatic Stress Disorder* (Princeton, NJ: Princeton University Press, 1995).

47. S. Eth and R. Pynoos, *Post-traumatic Stress Disorder in Children* (Los Angeles, CA: American Psychiatric Association, 1985).

48. D. Finkelhor, "Early and Long-term Effects of Child Sexual Abuse: An Update," *Professional Psychology: Research and Practice* 21 (1990): 325–30.

49. D. Finkelhor, "The Trauma of Child Sexual Abuse: Two Models," in *Lasting Effects of Child Sexual Abuse*, eds. G. E. Wyatt and G. J. Powell (Newbury Park, CA: Sage Publications, 1988), 61–82.

50. D. J. Gelinas, "The Persisting Negative Effects of Incest," *Psychiatry* 46 (1983): 312–32.

51. R. C. Summit, "The Child Sexual Abuse Accommodation Syndrome," *Child Abuse and Neglect* 7 (1983): 177–93, quote on 184.

52. J. E. Davis, *Accounts of Innocence*, 134.

53. B. Glassner, *The Culture of Fear: Why Americans Are Afraid of the Wrong Things* (New York: Basic Books, 2000).

54. For a review of how people misinterpret risks, see P. Taylor-Gooby and J. O. Zinn, *Risk in Social Science* (Oxford: Oxford University Press, 1996); D. Gardner, *The Science of Fear: Why We Fear the Things We Shouldn't—and Put Ourselves in Greater Danger* (New York: Dutton Adult, 2008).

55. D. A. Snow et al., "Frame Alignment Processes, Micromobilization, and Movement Participation," *American Sociological Review* 51 (1986): 464–81.

56. Herman, *Trauma and Recovery*, 32.

57. E. Bass and L. Davis, *The Courage to Heal: A Guide for Women Survivors of Child Sexual Abuse*, 4th ed. (New York: HarperCollins, 2008), xi.

CHAPTER FOUR: Why the Trauma Myth Damages Victims

1. T. R. Miller, M. A. Cohen, and B. Wiersema, *Victims Costs and Consequences: A New Look* (Washington DC: National Institute of Justice, 1996).

2. F. D. Fincham et al., "The Professional Response to Child Sexual Abuse: Whose Interests Are Served?" in *Child Sexual Abuse and False Memory Syndrome*, ed. R. A. Baker (Amherst, NY: Prometheus Books, 1998), 279–308.

3. For example, see E. A. Holman and R. C. Silver, "Is It Abuse or the Aftermath? A Stress and Coping Approach to Understanding Response to Incest," *Journal of Social and Clinical Psychology* 15 (1996): 318–39; E. B. Carlson et al., "A Conceptual Framework for the Long-term Psychological Effects of Traumatic Childhood Abuse," *Child Maltreatment* 2 (1997): 272–95; S. Spaccarelli, "Stress, Appraisal, and Coping in Child Sexual Abuse: A Theoretical and Empirical Review," *Psychological Bulletin* 116 (1994): 340–62.

4. M. L. Bowman, "Individual Differences in Posttraumatic Distress: Problems with the DSM-IV Model," *Canadian Journal of Psychiatry* 44 (1999): 21–33; C. R. Brewin, B. Andrews, and J. D. Valentine, "Meta-analysis of Risk Factors for Posttraumatic Stress Disorder in Trauma-Exposed Adults," *Journal of Consulting and Clinical Psychology* 68 (2000): 748–66.

5. S. L. Toth and D. Cicchetti, "Where Do We Go from Here in Our Treatment of Victims?" in *Child Development and Social Policy*, eds. D. Cicchetti and S. L. Toth (Norwood, NJ: Ablen, 1993), 399–437.

6. B. Shephard, *A War of Nerves: Soldiers and Psychiatrists in the 20th Century* (Cambridge, MA: Harvard University Press, 2000), 392.

7. C. R. Browning and E. O. Laumann, "Sexual Contact Between Children and Adults: A Life Course Perspective," *American Sociological Review* 62 (1997): 540–60; Spaccarelli, "Stress, Appraisal, and Coping in Child

Sexual Abuse"; D. Finkelhor, *Childhood Victimization: Violence, Crime, and Abuse in the Lives of Young People* (Oxford: Oxford University Press, 2008), 64–91.

8. D. C. Rubin, D. Berntsen, and M. K. Bohni, "A Memory-Based Model of Posttraumatic Stress Disorder: Evaluating Basic Assumptions Underlying the PTSD Diagnosis," *Psychological Review* 115 (2008): 985–1011.

9. D. Finkelhor, *Sexually Victimized Children* (New York: Free Press, 1979), 49.

10. L. Berliner and J. R. Conte, "The Process of Victimization: The Victims' Perspective," *Child Abuse and Neglect* 14 (1990): 29–40, quote on 34.

11. M. A. Epstein and B. L. Bottoms, "Explaining the Forgetting and Recovery of Abuse and Trauma Memories: Possible Mechanisms," *Child Maltreatment* 7 (2002): 210–25.

12. For a wonderful overview of the phenomenology of betrayal and a review of the research, see J. Freyd, *Betrayal Trauma* (Cambridge, MA: Harvard University Press, 1996).

13. M. Bard and D. Sangrey, *The Crime Victim's Book* (New York: Basic Books, 1979), 14–15.

14. R. Janoff-Bulman, *Shattered Assumptions: Towards a New Psychology of Trauma* (New York: Free Press, 1992).

15. S. E. Taylor, "Adjustment to Threatening Events: A Theory of Cognitive Adaptation," *American Psychologist* (1983): 1161–73; J. J. Kolko and C. Feiring, "Explaining Why: A Closer Look at Attributions in Child Abuse Victims," *Child Maltreatment* 7 (2002): 5–8.

16. F. C. Bartlett, *Remembering: A Study in Experimental and Social Psychology* (Cambridge: Cambridge University Press, 1932).

17. R. Janoff-Bulman and C. B. Wortman, "Attributions of Blame and Coping in the 'Real World': Severe Accident Victims React to Their Lot," *Journal of Personality and Social Psychology* 35 (1977): 351–63; R. Janoff-Bulman, *Shattered Assumptions: Towards a New Psychology of Trauma* (New York: The Free Press, 1992).

18. M. J. Lerner and C. H. Simmons, "Observer's Reactions to the 'Innocent Victim': Compassion or Rejection?" *Journal of Personality and Social Psychology* 4 (1966): 203–10, quote on 203.

19. P. T. Wong and B. Weiner, "When People Ask 'Why' Questions and the Heuristics of Attributional Search," *Journal of Personality and Social Psychology* 40 (1981): 650–63.

20. See, for example, F. Heider, *The Psychology of Interpersonal Relations* (New York: Wiley, 1958); C. Feiring, L. Taska, and K. Chen, "Trying to Understand Why Horrible Things Happen: Attribution, Shame, and

NOTES TO PAGES 131–33

Symptom Development Following Sexual Abuse," *Child Maltreatment* 7 (2002): 26–41.

21. L. Y. Abramson, M. E. Seligman, and J. D. Teasdale, "Learned Helplessness in Humans: Critique and Reformulation," *Journal of Abnormal Psychology* 87 (1978): 49–74; C. Peterson, G. M. Buchanan, and M. E. P. Seligman, "Explanatory Style: History and Evolution of the Field," in *Explanatory Style*, eds. G. M. Buchanan and M. E. Seligman (Hillsdale, NJ: Lawrence Erlbaum, 1995), 57–70; C. Peterson and M. E. Seligman, "Learned Helplessness and Victimization," *Journal of Social Issues* 39 (1983): 103–16.

22. L. Bender and A. Blau, "The Reaction of Children to Sexual Relations with Adults," *American Journal of Orthopsychiatry* 7 (1937): 500–18; P. Sloane and E. Karpinski, "Effects of Incest upon the Participants," *American Journal of Orthopsychiatry* 12 (1942): 666–74; M. Tsai, S. Feldman-Summers, and M. Edgar, "Childhood Molestation: Variables Related to Differential Impacts on Psychosexual Functioning in Adult Women," *Journal of Abnormal Psychology* 88 (1979): 407–17.

23. D. J. Gelinas, "The Persisting Negative Effects of Incest," *Psychiatry* 46 (1983): 312–31, quote on 322.

24. I. Kaufman, A. L. Peck, and C. K. Tagiuri, "The Family Constellation and Overt Incestuous Relations Between Father and Daughter," *American Journal of Orthopsychiatry* 24 (1954): 266–79.

25. Gelinas, "The Persisting Negative Effects of Incest," 322.

26. E. Bass and L. Davis, *The Courage to Heal: A Guide for Women Survivors of Child Sexual Abuse*, 4th ed. (New York: HarperCollins, 2008).

27. J. Herman, *Trauma and Recovery: The Aftermath of Violence—from Domestic Abuse to Political Terror* (New York: Basic Books, 1992).

28. Bass and Davis, *The Courage to Heal*.

29. D. Spiegel, "Suffer the Children: Longterm Effects of Sexual Abuse," *Society* 4 (2000): 18–20. For further discussion, see C. Feiring, L. Taska, and M. Lewis, "The Role of Shame and Attributional Style in Children's and Adolescents' Adaptation to Sexual Abuse," *Child Maltreatment* 3 (1998): 129–42.

30. For a discussion of the proposed diagnosis of complex posttraumatic stress disorder, see Herman, *Trauma and Recovery*, 115–29.

31. B. Rind, P. Tromovitch, and R. Bauserman, "Condemnation of a Scientific Article: A Chronology and Refutation of the Attacks and a Discussion of Threats to the Integrity of Science," *Sexuality & Culture: An Interdisciplinary Quarterly* 4 (2000): 1–62; D. Spiegel, "Who Is in Procrustes's Bed?" *Sexuality & Culture: An Interdisciplinary Quarterly* 5 (2001): 78–86; B.

220

Rind, R. Bauserman, and P. Tromovitch, "Moralistic Psychiatry, Procrustes' Bed, and the Science of Child Sexual Abuse: A Response to Spiegel," *Sexuality & Culture* 5 (2001): 79–89.

32. S. A. Burkhardt and A. F. Rotatori, *Treatment and Prevention of Child Sexual Abuse: A Child-Generated Model* (Washington, DC: Taylor & Francis, 1995).

33. For additional support, see K. McFarlane, "Sexual Abuse of Children" in *The Victimization of Women*, eds. J. R. Chapman and M. Gates (Beverly Hills, CA: Sage Publications, 1978).

34. C. G. Davis et al., "Self-blame Following a Traumatic Event: The Role of Perceived Avoidability," *Personality and Social Psychology Bulletin* 22 (1996): 557–67.

35. For a discussion of how people use available information (incorrectly) to determine the cause of negative events, see S. A. Clancy, *Abducted: How People Come to Believe They Were Kidnapped by Aliens* (Cambridge, MA: Harvard University Press, 2005).

36. For a discussion of how the media's portrayal of sexual abuse impacts beliefs in the general population, see J. Kitzinger, *Framing Abuse: Media Influences and Public Understanding of Sexual Violence Against Children* (London: Pluto Press, 2004).

37. E. S. Blume, *Secret Survivors: Uncovering Incest and Its Aftereffects in Women* (New York: Ballantine, 1985).

38. F. Rush, "The Freudian Cover-up," *Chrysalis* 1 (1977): 31–45, quote on 42.

39. J. L. Herman, *Father-Daughter Incest* (Cambridge, MA: Harvard University Press, 1981), 186.

40. K. C. Meiselman, *Resolving the Trauma of Incest: Reintegration Therapy with Survivors* (San Francisco: Jossey-Bass, 1990), 72.

41. Bass and Davis, *The Courage to Heal.*

42. E. Deblinger and M. Runyon, "Understanding and Treating Feelings of Shame in Children Who Have Experienced Maltreatment," *Child Maltreatment* 10 (2005): 364–76; B. Andrews, "Bodily Shame As a Mediator Between Abusive Experiences and Depression," *Journal of Abnormal Psychology* 104 (1995): 277–85; C. Negrao et al., "Shame, Humiliation, and Childhood Sexual Abuse: Distinct Contributions and Emotional Coherence," *Child Maltreatment: Journal of the American Professional Society on the Abuse of Children* 10 (2005): 350–63.

43. D. W. Harder and S. J. Lewis, "The Assessment of Shame and Guilt," in *Advances in Personality Assessment*, eds. J. N. Butcher and C. D. Spielberger (Hillsdale, NJ: Lawrence Erlbaum), 89–114.

44. S. Spaccarelli, "Stress, Appraisal, and Coping in Child Sexual Abuse"; Browning and Laumann, "Sexual Contact Between Children and Adults"; Finkelhor, *Childhood Victimization.*

45. Feiring, Taska, and Lewis, "The Role of Shame"; B. Andrews et al., "Predicting PTSD Symptoms in Victims of Violent Crime: The Role of Shame, Anger, and Childhood Abuse," *Journal of Abnormal Psychology* 109 (2000): 69–73; F. E. Mennen, "Evaluation of Risk Factors in Childhood Sexual Abuse," *Journal of the American Academy of Child and Adolescent Psychiatry* 32 (1993): 934–39; M. P. Celano, "A Developmental Model of Victims' Internal Attributions of Responsibility for Sexual Abuse," *Journal of Interpersonal Violence* 7 (1992): 57–69.

46. A. McDonagh et al., "Randomized Trial of Cognitive-Behavioral Therapy for Chronic Posttraumatic Stress Disorder in Adult Female Survivors of Childhood Sexual Abuse," *Journal of Consulting and Clinical Psychology* 73 (2005): 515–24; A. T. Moller and H. R. Steel, "Clinically Significant Change After Cognitive Restructuring for Adult Survivors of Childhood Sexual Abuse," *Journal of Rational-Emotive and Cognitive Behavior Therapy* 20 (2002): 49–64; P. Ramchandani and D. P. H. Jones, "Treating Psychological Symptoms in Sexually Abused Children: From Research Findings to Service Provision," *British Journal of Psychiatry* 183 (2003): 484–90; M. Celano et al., "Attribution Retraining with Sexually Abused Children: Review of Techniques," *Child Maltreatment* 7 (2002): 64–75.

47. C. J. Dalenberg and D. A. Jacobs, "Attributional Analysis of Child Sexual Abuse Episodes: Empirical and Clinical Issues," *Journal of Child Sexual Abuse* 3 (1994): 37–50; S. Lamb, "Treating Sexually Abused Children: Issues of Blame and Responsibility," *American Journal of Orthopsychiatry* 56 (1986): 303–7.

CHAPTER FIVE: How the Trauma Myth Silences Victims

1. F. Rush, "The Freudian Cover-up," *Crysalis* 1 (1971): 45; S. Butler, *A Conspiracy of Silence* (San Francisco: New Glide, 1978).

2. M. L. Paine and D. J. Hansen, "Factors Influencing Children to Self-disclose Sexual Abuse," *Clinical Psychology Review* 22 (2002): 271–95; G. Priebe and C. G. Svedin,"Child Sexual Abuse Is Largely Hidden from Adult Society," *Child Abuse and Neglect* 12 (2008): 1095–1108.

3. R. F. Hanson et al., "Factors Relating to the Reporting of Childhood Rape," *Child Abuse and Neglect* 23 (1999): 559–69.

4. E. O. Laumann et al., *The Social Organization of Sexuality: Sexual Practices in the United States* (Chicago: University of Chicago Press, 1994).

5. E. S. Blume, *Secret Survivors: Uncovering Incest and Its Aftereffects in Women* (New York: Random House, 1990); E. Bass and L. Davis, *The Courage to Heal: A Guide for Women Survivors of Child Sexual Abuse*, 4th ed. (New York: HarperCollins, 2008).

6. Bass and Davis, *The Courage to Heal*, 104.

7. Blume, *Secret Survivors*, 65.

8. J. L. Herman, *Father-Daughter Incest* (Cambridge, MA: Harvard University Press, 1981), quotes on 88.

9. N. D. Kellogg and T. J. Hoffman, "Unwanted and Illegal Sexual Experiences in Childhood and Adolescence," *Child Abuse and Neglect* 19 (1995): 1457–68; N. D. Kellogg and R. L. Huston, "Unwanted Sexual Experiences in Adolescents: Patterns of Disclosure," *Clinical Pediatrics* 34 (1995): 306–12; S. M. Kogan, "Disclosing Unwanted Sexual Experiences: Results from a National Sample of Adolescent Women," *Child Abuse and Neglect* 28 (2004): 147–65; Hanson et al., "Factors Related to the Reporting of Childhood Rape."

10. R. Cheit, quoted in J. J. Freyd, *Betrayal Trauma* (Cambridge, MA: Harvard University Press, 1997), 59.

11. Bass and Davis, *The Courage to Heal*, xxix.

12. J. W. Pennebaker, *Emotions, Disclosure, and Health* (Washington, DC: American Psychological Association, 1995); J. M. Smyth, "Written Emotional Expression: Effect Sizes, Outcome Type, and Moderating Variables," *Journal of Consulting and Clinical Psychology* 66 (1998): 174–84.

13. D. Finkelhor and L. Berliner, "Research on the Treatment of Sexually Abused Children: A Review and Recommendations," *Journal of the American Academy of Child and Adolescent Psychiatry* 34 (1995): 1408–23; N. L. Talbott, "Women Sexually Abused As Children: The Centrality of Shame Issues and Treatment Implications," *Psychotherapy Theory, Research, Practice, Training* 33 (1996): 11–18.

14. W. Koutstaal and D. L. Schacter, "Intentional Forgetting and Voluntary Thought Suppression: Two Potential Methods for Coping with Childhood Trauma," in *Review of Psychiatry*, eds. L. J. Dickstein, M. B. Riba, and J. M. Oldham, 16 (1997): 79–121 (Washington: American Psychiatric Press); H. Leitenberg, E. Greenwald, and S. Cado, "A Retrospective Study of Long-Term Methods of Coping with Having Been Sexually Abused During Childhood," *Child Abuse and Neglect* 16 (1992): 399–407; M. A. Epstein and B. L. Bottoms, "Explaining the Forgetting and Recovery of Abuse and Trauma Memories: Possible Mechanisms," *Child Maltreatment* 7 (2002): 210–25.

15. R. J. McNally and E. Geraerts, "A New Solution to the Recovered Memory Debate," *Perspectives on Psychological Science* 4 (2009): 126–34.

16. S. A. Clancy et al., "False Recognition in Women Reporting Recovered Memories of Sexual Abuse," *Psychological Science* 11 (2000): 26–31; R. J. McNally et al., "Clinical Characteristics of Adults Reporting Repressed, Recovered and Continuous Memories of Childhood Sexual Abuse," *Journal of Consulting and Clinical Psychology* 74 (2006): 237–42.

17. The last quote is from L. Armstrong, *Kiss Daddy Goodnight* (New York: Pocket Books, 1979), 259–60.

18. D. L. Schacter, K. A. Norman, and W. Koutstaal, "The Cognitive Neuroscience of Reconstructive Memory," *Annual Review of Psychology* 49 (1998): 289–318; D. L. Schacter, *The Seven Sins of Memory: How the Mind Forgets and Remembers* (Boston: Houghton Mifflin, 2001).

19. J. Silverman and D. Wilson, *Innocence Betrayed: Paedophilia, the Media and Society* (Oxford: Blackwell Publishing, 2002); D. J. Whitaker et al., "Risk Factors for the Perpetration of Child Sexual Abuse," *Child Abuse and Neglect* 32 (2008): 529–48.

20. Today, although as many as 30 percent of girls and 15 percent of boys are sexually abused in childhood, only a small number of these cases are identified each year. Even if they are identified, less than one in five identified offenders is convicted, and less than a third of those convicted spend more than a year in jail. For a review of data pertaining to this topic, see R. M. Bolen, *Child Sexual Abuse: Its Scope and Our Failure* (New York: Kluwer Academic/Plenum Publishers, 2001).

21. Bass and Davis, *The Courage to Heal*, 102, 104.

22. Russell, *The Secret Trauma*.

23. R. J. McNally, *Remembering Trauma* (Cambridge, MA: Belknap Press, 2003); D. Brown, A. W. Scheflin, and D. C. Hammond, *Memory, Trauma Treatment, and the Law* (New York: W. W. Norton & Company, 1998).

24. K. K. Shobe and J. F. Kihlstrom, "Is Traumatic Memory Special?" *Current Directions in Psychological Science* 7 (1997): 154–56.

25. E. Loftus and K. Ketcham, *The Myth of Repressed Memory: False Memories and Allegations of Sexual Abuse* (New York: St. Martin's Griffin, 1994); H. G. Pope et al., "Questionable Validity of 'Dissociative Amnesia' in Trauma Victims," *British Journal of Psychiatry* 172 (1998): 210–15; R. J. McNally, "The Science and Folklore of Traumatic Amnesia," *Clinical Psychology: Science and Practice* 11 (2004): 29–33.

26. Gen. 19: 30–36.

27. V. Nabokov, *Lolita* (New York: Berkley Medallion, 1966), 122–23.

28. L. Bender and A. Blau, "The Reaction of Children to Sexual Relations with Adults," *American Journal of Orthopsychiatry* 7 (1937): 500–18, quote on 514.

29. R. A. Hibbard and T. W. Zollinger, "Patterns of Child Sexual Abuse Knowledge Among Professionals," *Child Abuse and Neglect* 14 (1990): 347–55; S. Morison and E. Greene, "Juror and Expert Knowledge of Child Sexual Abuse," *Child Abuse and Neglect* 16 (1992): 595–613; M. B. Kovera et al., "Do Child Sexual Abuse Experts Hold Pro-Child Beliefs? A Survey of the International Society for Traumatic Stress Studies," *Journal of Traumatic Stress* 6 (1993): 383–404; Bolen, *Child Sexual Abuse*.

30. Bolen, *Child Sexual Abuse*, 222.

31. L. Bensley et al., "General Population Norms About Child Abuse and Neglect and Associations with Childhood Experiences," *Child Abuse and Neglect* 28 (2004): 1321–37; C. MacMartin, "Judicial Constructions of the Seriousness of Child Sexual Abuse," *Canadian Journal of Behavioral Science* 36 (2004): 66–80; R. L. Shackel, "The Beliefs Commonly Held by Adults About Children's Behavioral Responses to Sexual Abuse," *Child Abuse and Neglect* 32, no. 4 (2008): 484–95.

32. Rush, "The Freudian Cover-up," 43.

33. J. B. Kaplow et al., "Pathways to PTSD, Part II: Sexually Abused Children," *American Journal of Psychiatry* 162 (2005): 1305–10.

34. J. R. Conte and J. R. Schuerman, "Factors Associated with an Increased Impact of Child Sexual Abuse," *Child Abuse and Neglect* 11 (1987): 201–11; M. D. Everson et al. "Maternal Support Following Disclosure of Incest," *American Journal of Orthopsychiatry* 59 (1989): 197–207; B. B. Lovett, "Child Sexual Abuse Disclosure: Maternal Response and Other Variables Impacting the Victim," *Child and Adolescent Social Work Journal* 21 (2004): 355–71; H. Kouyoumdjian, A. R. Perry, and D. J. Hansen, "The Role of Adult Expectations in the Recovery of Sexually Abused Children," *Aggression and Violent Behavior* 10 (2005): 475–89.

35. H. F. Harlow, "Love in Infant Monkeys," *Scientific American* 200 (1959): 68–74.

36. M. A. Novak and H. F. Harlow, "Social Recovery of Monkey's Isolated for the First Year of Life: Rehabilitation and Therapy," *Developmental Psychology* 1 (1979): 50–61.

37. J. Bowlby, *A Secure Base: Parent-Child Attachment and Healthy Human Development* (New York: Basic Books, 1988).

38. M. Klein, *The Writings of Melanie Klein*, vol. 3 (London: Hogarth Press, 1975); O. Kernberg, *Object Relations Theory and Clinical Psychoanalysis* (New York: Jason Aronson, 1976); H. Kohut, "Selected Problems of Self-psychological Theory," in *Reflections of Self Psychology*, eds. J. D. Lichtenberg and S. Kaplan (Hillsdale, NJ: Erlbaum Associates, 1983), 387–416.

39. Bensley et al., "General Population Norms"; M. E. Collins, "Parents' Perceptions of the Risk of Child Sexual Abuse and Their Protective Behaviors: Findings from a Qualitative Study," *Child Maltreatment* 1 (1996): 53–64; Shackel, "The Beliefs Commonly Held by Adults."

40. One of the most prominent critics has been David Finkelhor. Since his first book in 1979, *Sexually Victimized Children*, he has been arguing against the application of the PTSD conceptualization to child sexual abuse. The fact that in his most recent book, *Childhood Sexual Victimization* (2008), his concerns remain relatively unchanged is, I believe, strong evidence that the field has been slow to change its conceptualizations about sexual abuse and its damaging effects.

41. Rush, "The Freudian Cover-up," 45.

CONCLUSION

1. R. J. McNally, "The Demise of Pseudoscience," *The Scientific Review of Mental Health Practice* 2 (2003): 97–101, quote on 97.

2. C. Sagan, *The Demon-Haunted World: Science As a Candle in the Dark* (1996; rpt. New York: Ballantine, 1997), 39.

3. M. A. Hagan, "Faith in the Model and Resistance to Research," *Clinical Psychology: Science and Practice* 10 (2003): 344–48, quote on 344.

4. B. Rind, P. Tromovitch, and R. Bauserman, "A Meta-analytic Examination of Assumed Properties of Child Sexual Abuse Using College Samples," *Psychological Bulletin* 124 (1998): 22–53.

5. S. O. Lilienfeld, "When Worlds Collide: Social Science, Politics, and the Rind et al. (1998). Child Sexual Abuse Meta-analysis," *American Psychologist* 57, no. 3 (2002): 176–88; B. Rind, P. Tromovitch, and R. Bauserman, "Condemnation of a Scientific Article: A Chronology and Refutation of the Attacks and a Discussion of Threats to the Integrity of Science," *Sexuality & Culture: An Interdisciplinary Quarterly* 4 (2000): 1–62; D. Spiegel, "Who Is in Procrustes's Bed?" *Sexuality & Culture: An Interdisciplinary Quarterly* 5 (2001): 78–86; B. Rind, R. Bauserman, and P. Tromovitch, "Moralistic Psychiatry, Procrustes' Bed, and the Science of Child Sexual Abuse: A Response to Spiegel," *Sexuality & Culture* 5 (2001): 79–89.

6. U.S. House of Representatives, Concurrent Resolution 107 of the 106th Congress, July 12, 1999.

7. I. Lerch, "Letter from the Chair of the American Association for the Advancement of Science's Committee on Scientific Freedom and Responsibility to Richard McCarty, Executive Director of Science, American Psychological Association," *Psychological Science Agenda* 12 (November–December 1999): 2–3.

8. For a review of cognitive and developmental factors that preclude children's recognition and effective response to these crimes, see S. A. Burkhardt and A. F. Rotatori, *Treatment and Prevention of Childhood Sexual Abuse: A Child-Generated Model* (Washington, DC: Taylor & Francis, 1995).

9. C. Tavris, "The Uproar over Sexual Abuse Research and its Findings," *Society* (May–June 2000): 15–17, quote on 16.

10. For support for a stronger ethical position on the matter of child sexual abuse, one less dependent on the presumption of harm, see D. Finkelhor, "What's Wrong with Sex Between Adults and Children? Ethics and the Problem of Sexual Abuse," *American Journal of Orthopsychiatry* 49 (1979): 692–97.

11. J. L. Herman, *Father-Daughter Incest* (1981; rpt. Cambridge, MA: Harvard University Press, 2000), 4.

12. There was an explosion of research in the 1980s on cognitive consistency theories. In particular, cognitive dissonance theory demonstrated people's strong motivation to maintain congruence in their attitudes and behavior, especially in those most related to their self-concept. For a recent review and discussion, see C. Tavris and E. Aronson, *Mistakes Were Made (But Not by Me): Why We Justify Foolish Beliefs, Bad Decisions, and Hurtful Acts* (Orlando, FL: Harcourt, 2007).

13. For a review of the development of the trauma theory, see J. E. Davis, *Accounts of Innocence: Sexual Abuse, Trauma, and the Self* (Chicago: University of Chicago Press, 2005).

14. National Research Council, *Understanding Child Abuse and Neglect* (Washington, DC: National Academy Press, 1993).

15. The following 1996 report from the Department of Justice estimates that the rape and sexual abuse of children cost U.S. victims $23 billion total annually: T. R. Miller, M. A. Cohen, and B. Wiersema, *Victim Costs and Consequences: A New Look* (Washington, DC: U.S. Department of Justice, 1996).

16. D. Finkelhor, "The Victimization of Children: A Developmental Perspective," *American Journal of Orthopsychiatry* 65 (1995): 177–93; S. Spaccarelli, "Stress, Appraisal, and Coping in Child Sexual Abuse: A Theoretical and Empirical Review," *Psychological Bulletin* 116 (1994): 340–62; D. Finkelhor, *Childhood Victimization: Violence, Crime, and Abuse in the Lives of Young People* (Oxford: Oxford University Press, 2008).

17. For an early and tremendously influential paper on child victims' failure to disclose, see R. C. Summit, "The Child Sexual Abuse Accommodation Syndrome," *Child Abuse and Neglect* 7 (1983): 177–93.

18. There is no definitive source for state statute of limitations applicable to civil claims of child sexual abuse. A recent state-by-state survey

(and other resources for sexual-abuse victims) can be found at www.smith
-lawfirm.com.

19. Nearly every state has a basic extension for its statute of limitations. These extensions are based on the "delayed discovery" rule. Delayed
discovery may be due to repression (caused by the psychological trauma
of the abuse experience when it happened) or by the victims' only belatedly
realizing that the abuse caused psychological or physical injuries.
Explicit and implicit in both the statute of limitations and delayed discovery is the assumption that for sexual abuse to be a crime, it must have been
traumatic when it happened and/or harmful. This is unfair to victims.
Sexual abuse is criminal and wrong regardless of whether it was traumatic for the victims or subsequently damaging.

20. R. J. McNally and E. Geraerts, "A New Solution to the Recovered
Memory Debate," *Perspectives on Psychological Science* 4 (2009): 126–34.

21. Further, many victims find the experiences unpleasant or shameful
and report trying to forget them. Some research indicates that purposely
suppressing information may lead to its subsequently being forgotten. For
example, see M. C. Anderson and C. Green, "Suppressing Unwanted
Memories by Executive Control," *Nature* 410 (2001): 366–69.

22. For what is arguably the definitive review on the scientific support
for recovered memory, see R. J. McNally, *Remembering Trauma* (Cambridge, MA: Belknap Press, 2003).

23. D. Finkelhor, N. Asdigian, and J. Dziuba-Leatherman, "Victimization Prevention Programs for Children: A Follow-up," *American Journal of
Public Health* 85 (1995): 1684–89; R. M. Bolen, "Child Sexual Abuse: Prevention or Promotion?" *Social Work* 48 (2003): 174–85.

24. D. Finkelhor, N. Asdigian, and J. Dziuba-Leatherman, "The Effec-
tiveness of Victimization Prevention Instruction: An Evaluation of Children's Responses to Actual Threats and Assaults," *Child Abuse and Neglect*
19 (1995): 141–53.

25. S. K. Wurtele and C. L. Miller-Perrin, *Preventing Child Sexual Abuse:
Sharing the Responsibility* (Lincoln: University of Nebraska Press, 1992); J.
L. Olsen and C. S. Widom, "Prevention of Child Abuse and Neglect," *Ap-
plied and Preventive Psychology* 2 (1993): 217–29; Burkhardt and Rotatori,
Treatment and Prevention of Childhood Sexual Abuse; D. Finkelhor and D.
Daro, "Prevention of Child Sexual Abuse," in *The Battered Child*, eds.
M. E. Helfer, R. S. Kempe, and R. D. Krugman, 5th ed. (Chicago: Univer-
sity of Chicago Press, 1997), 615–26.

26. G. B. Melton, foreword to Wurtele and Miller-Perrin, *Preventing
Child Sexual Abuse*, ix.

27. Quoted in Bolen, "Child Sexual Abuse," 174–85.

28. D. Reiss and R. H. Price, "National Research Agenda for Prevention Research," *American Psychologist* 51 (1996): 1109–15; P. M. McMahon and R. C. Puett, "Child Sexual Abuse As a Public Health Issue," *Sexual Abuse: A Journal of Research and Treatment* 11 (1999): 257–66; V. L. Banyard, E. G. Plante, and M. M. Moynihan, "Bystander Education: Bringing a Broader Community Perspective to Sexual Violence Prevention," *Journal of Community Psychology* 32 (2004): 61–79; A. Boehm and H. Itzhaky, "The Social Marketing Approach: A Way to Increase Reporting and Treatment of Sexual Assault," *Child Abuse and Neglect* 28 (2004): 253–65.

29. David Finkelhor convincingly argues that people in general are very resistant to accepting the notion that perpetrators are, in most cases, not strangers but rather people we know and trust. Family life, friendships, and social networks cannot operate without trust and assumptions of reciprocity. Education can help people recognize the dangers close at hand, but people may never overcome the tendency to underestimate these risks or learn to instinctively put family members ahead of strangers in their risk hierarchy. See Finkelhor, *Childhood Victimization.*

30. J. K. Galbraith, *The Affluent Society* (New York: Houghton Mifflin, 1958).

31. B. Glassner, *The Culture of Fear: Why Americans Are Afraid of the Wrong Things* (New York: Basic Books, 1999).

32. J. Herman and L. Hirschman, "Father-Daughter Incest," *Signs* 2 (1977): 1–22; S. Butler, *Conspiracy of Silence* (San Francisco: New Glide, 1978); L. Armstrong, *Kiss Daddy Goodnight* (New York: Hawthorn, 1978); F. Rush, *The Best-Kept Secret: Sexual Abuse of Children* (New York: McGraw-Hill, 1980).

33. R. C. Summit, "Hidden Victims, Hidden Pain: Society's Avoidance of Child Sexual Abuse," in *Lasting Effects of Child Sexual Abuse*, eds. G. E. Wyatt and G. J. Powell (Newbury Park, CA: Sage Publications, 1988), 39–60; E. Olafson, D. L. Corwin, and R. C. Summit, "Modern History of Child Sexual Abuse Awareness: Cycles of Discovery and Suppression," *Child Abuse and Neglect* 17 (1993): 7–24, quote on 24.

34. P. McHugh, "Psychiatric Misadventures," *The American Scholar* 61 (1992): 497–510, quotes on 501, 510.

INDEX

Abraham, Karl, 69, 84–85
Accounts of Innocence (Davis), 102
Against Our Will (Brownmiller),
 92
Alcohol and drug abuse, 4, 19,
 50, 95, 96, 101
American Academy of Child and
 Adolescent Psychiatry, 11
American Association for the
 Advancement of Science
 (AAAS), 183
American Psychological
 Association, 182
Angelou, Maya, 71–72
Anxiety, 4, 9, 61, 96, 100, 115
Aristotle, 127

Bard, Morton, 123
Bartlett, Frederick, 128
"The Battered-Child Syndrome"
 (Kempe), 87
Bender, Lauretta, 85, 131, 165
Benford, Robert, 106
Berliner, Lucy, 66, 70–71, 120
Best, Joel, 93
Blau, Abram, 131
Bolen, Rebecca, 166
Boston Globe, 20
Bottoms, Bette, 120–121
Bowlby, John, 172
Breuer, Josef, 17
Brown, Angela, 95

Brownmiller, Susan, 92
Burkhard, Sandra, 64

Cambridge Hospital, 47, 48, 49,
 78
Carlson, Eve, 61
Center for Child Victimization,
 61
Cheating detection, 68–69
Cheit, Ross, 68, 153–154
Child Abuse and Neglect (journal),
 93
Child development and
 cognition, 63–64, 65–66,
 69, 70, 184, 193
*A Child-Generated Model of Sexual
 Abuse* (Burkhard and
 Rotatori), 64
Child-protection advocates and
 movement, 87, 93, 96, 99,
 106, 165, 199
Child sexual abuse. *See* Sexual
 abuse, child
Childhood Victimization
 (Finkelhor), 113
Combat, 12, 18, 97, 98, 114
Conte, Jon, 66, 120
Cosmides, Leda, 68
The Courage to Heal (book),
 13–14, 107, 139, 151
The Culture of Fear (Glassner),
 103, 199

Davis, Joseph, 79, 102
De Francis, Vincent, 88
Depression, 4, 9, 19, 22, 50, 51,
    96, 115, 143
The Dialectic of Sex (Firestone),
    88
Dissociation, 54–55, 56, 62

Eating disorders, 4, 95
Epstein, Michelle, 120–121

Family Research Center
    (University of New
    Hampshire), 63
Feminists
    and blaming children, 89, 90,
        91, 92, 164, 165
    come out against sexual abuse,
        88–92, 93, 94, 199–200
    and psychological problems,
        96
    and PTSD, 99
    and silence of victims, 149–150
    and trauma theory, 106
Finkelhor, David, 60, 61, 66, 95,
    113, 119–120
Firestone, Shulamith, 88
Fliess, Wilhelm, 81
Freud, Sigmund, 17, 81–82, 84,
    127
"Freudian Cover-up" (Rush), 89

Gagnon, John, 59–60, 83
Galbraith, John Kenneth, 198–
    199
Gelinas, Denise, 11, 100, 131
Glassner, Barry, 103, 104, 199
Good Touch Bad Touch (book),
    194

Hacking, Ian, 79, 80
Hagan, Margaret, 62, 182

Harlow, Harry, 171
The Harmony of Illusions (Young),
    98
Harvard Medical School, 10, 47,
    54, 77
Harvard University, 21, 47, 52,
    77
Herman, Judith
    and consent, 139
    and exploitation of children by
        protectors, 186
    and feminists, 91–92
    and guilt, 132
    study with Hirschman on
        females molested by
        fathers, 70
    and trauma theory, 9–10,
        11–12, 18, 106
Hirschman, Linda, 70

I Know Why the Caged Bird Sings
    (Angelou), 71
"Incest: Sexual Abuse Begins at
    Home" (Weber), 93–94
International Society for the
    Study of Posttraumatic
    Stress, 98

James, William, 127
Janoff-Bulman, Ronnie, 128
Jenkins, Philip, 83
*Journal of the American Medical
    Association*, 87
Journal of Traumatic Stress, 98
Justice, U.S. Department of, 111

Karpman, Benjamin, 86
Kaufmann, Irving, 131
Kempe, C. Henry, 83, 87
Kendall-Tacket, Kathleen, 62
Kinsey, Alfred, 58, 60, 81

INDEX

Landis, Carney, 59
Landis, Judson, 58, 72
Lerner, M. J., 128
Limbaugh, Rush, 182
Lolita (Nabokov), 85, 164–165

Maastricht, University of, 59
Maher, Brendan, 127
McHugh, Paul, 202
McLean Hospital, 47
McNally, Richard, 17, 180, 192
Meiselman, Karin, 80, 139
Memory
    and avoidance and
        suppression, 155–156
    inaccurate, 52–55, 116, 192
    recovered, 14, 16–18, 191
    repressed, 16–18, 22, 161–162
Mood disorders, 4, 95
Mystic River (movie), 15

Nabokov, Vladimir, 164
National Center on Child Abuse
    and Neglect, 105
National Health and Social Life
    Survey, 150
National Institute of Mental
    Health, 51
National Research Council, 187
Natural disasters, 12, 98, 114
New York Radical Feminists, 88,
    90
Nixon, Richard, 103

Occam's razor, 55–56
Okami, Paul, 58
Olafson, Karen, 86

Pennebaker, James, 155
Piaget, Jean, 65
Pinker, Steven, 65
Popper, Karl, 65

Posttraumatic stress disorder
    (PTSD), 56
    complex, 132
    enters psychiatric diagnostic
        system, 98–99
    and memory, 17, 53, 54
    and sexual abuse, 4, 22, 50, 51,
        54, 61–62, 99–101, 102, 143
    and sexual abuse: reporting,
        170
Psychological Bulletin (journal),
    182
Psychosis, 4, 9, 95

Rape
    and feminists, 90, 91–92
    and minimization, 168
    and PTSD, 61, 100
    reporting, 151
    and sexual abuse, 12, 13, 14,
        15, 91–92, 93, 138
    and trauma theory, 98, 103,
        138
Repression, 17, 54, 62, 155
    See also Memory: repressed
Rind, Bruce, 182
Rotatori, Anthony, 64
Rush, Florence, 89, 90, 138–139,
    150, 170, 177–178
Russell, Diane, 60, 62

Sagan, Carl, 75, 181
Sangrey, Dawn, 123
Schacter, Daniel, 17
Schlessinger, Dr. Laura, 182
Scientific American (journal), 171
Searching for Memory (book), 52
Secret Survivors (book), 138, 151
The Secret Trauma (Russell), 60,
    62
Self-mutilation, 4, 9, 95
Seligman, Martin, 129